PENGUIN HANDBOOKS

GREAT BREAD!

Bernice Hunt is an enthusiastic baker of bread. "People refuse to believe me when I tell them that it's so easy to bake bread that anyone can do it, and that baking bread is exciting, intensely pleasurable, creative, unfailingly rewarding—and foolproof. In addition, it impresses a lot of people!" A children's book editor who has also taught creative writing in a university, she has written over sixty books for both adults and children, including *Marriage, The Divorce Experience* (with Morton Hunt), *Intimate Partners* (with Clifford Sager, M.D.), *The Spirit and the Letter, The Organic Living Book*, and *The Beach-comber's Book*. Articles by her have appeared in *Woman's Day, Family Circle, Redbook, Ladies' Home Journal,* and *Reader's Digest.* Mrs. Hunt lives with her husband, author Morton Hunt, in Bedford, New York. They write together and separately and take turns baking the bread as well.

BERNICE HUNT

GREAT BREAD!

The Easiest Possible Way to Make Almost 100 Kinds

Illustrated by Lauren Jarrett

PENGUIN BOOKS

**For Morton, the fastest knead in the East—
and Marty, the sourdough sage**

*Penguin Books Ltd, Harmondsworth,
Middlesex, England
Penguin Books, 625 Madison Avenue,
New York, New York 10022, U.S.A.
Penguin Books Australia Ltd, Ringwood,
Victoria, Australia
Penguin Books Canada Limited, 2801 John Street,
Markham, Ontario, Canada L3R 1B4
Penguin Books (N.Z.) Ltd, 182–190 Wairau Road,
Auckland 10, New Zealand*

*First published in the United States of America by
The Viking Press 1977
First published in Canada by
The Macmillan Company of Canada Limited 1977
Published in Penguin Books 1980
Reprinted 1981*

LIBRARY OF CONGRESS CATALOGING IN PUBLICATION DATA
Hunt, Bernice Kohn. Great bread! Includes index.
SUMMARY: *A brief history of bread, with a discussion of the traditional
ingredients and baking methods, introduces a variety of recipes
with the measurements given in both the metric and English system.
1. Bread. 2. Baking. I. Jarrett, Lauren. III. Title.
TX769.H83   1980   641.8'15   80-19124
ISBN 0 14 046.472 7*

*Printed in the United States of America by
Halliday Lithograph Corporation, West Hanover, Massachusetts
Set in Video Compano*

❧ Contents ❧

The History of Bread

Crush some seeds between two rocks. Mix the seeds with enough water to make a dough. Pat the dough into a flat cake and put it on a flat rock in the sun to bake.

BREAD

There was no written language when the first bread was baked, but if there had been, the original recipe might have read something like this one. Of course, we can't be sure.

The first bread we *can* be sure about was only a little bit more sophisticated than the sun-baked flatbread in the fictional recipe above, and it was made by the Neolithic Lake Dwellers about eight thousand years ago. These ancient people lived in what is now Switzerland; their lake-shore houses were built on stilts. The local waters were rich in minerals, and when some of the Lake Dwellers' settlements were flooded, chemicals in the water petrified many of the objects that were in use at the time. As a result, we know in extraordinary detail how these people lived—and one of the things we know about them is that they baked bread.

When modern archaeologists discovered one particular village, they found rock-hard loaves of flatbread sitting exactly where they had been left (to cool, perhaps?) by a Stone Age baker. From the evidence, it appears that the Lake Dwellers cleared fields and planted millet, barley, oats, rye, and wheat. They probably ground the cereals between stones and mixed the resulting coarse flour with water to form a dough. After they had shaped the dough into flat loaves, they placed it on rocks and covered it with hot ashes to bake.

From that modest beginning, bread has become the staple food of the Western world, and of much of the rest of the world as well. It is so important that many peoples use the word "bread" to signify all food. In English we say, "Give us this day our daily bread," "the family breadwinner," "earn your bread," "break bread with friends," and so forth.

There are many references to bread in the Bible, and the next chapter in the broken history of bread comes from this source. We learn in Genesis that "Lot made a feast and did bake unleavened bread," and in Exodus we read that the Jews fled Egypt in such a hurry that they had no time to let their bread rise. Jewish people all over the world commemorate that event by eating unleavened bread, *matzoh,* during the spring feast of Passover.

Because there are so many references to *un*leavened bread in the Old Testament, it is perfectly clear that the Hebrews knew how to make leavened, or risen, bread. They raised their dough with fermented grain, or sourdough starter—a fascinating procedure still in use today (*see* page 91). Bread was sufficiently important by Biblical times for most houses to have ovens in their yards; we can imagine the women sitting beside them in the sun, grinding the grain with stones.

Bread-baking was basic to life all over the Fertile Crescent (the valleys of the Tigris and Euphrates Rivers in what is now Iraq) and farther to the East, in the Indus River valley. As early as 4000 B.C. the people of these areas ate a pancake-shaped bread made of barley, sesame seeds, and onions. A similar bread is still made by Iraqi peasants, and flatbreads of various sorts are common throughout the region.

Simple flatbread was the only kind known for many years, but sometime before 3000 B.C. the Egyptians dramatically changed bread-baking from a standard, mundane procedure into a fine art. We have some knowledge of Egyptian bread because many of the tombs of the Pharaohs in the Valley of the Kings have elaborate drawings that show bread being offered to the gods. Forty different kinds of loaves can be found in the pictures: they are round, flat, long and thin, conical, spiral, triangular—and combinations and variations of all these besides. The Metropolitan Museum of Art in New York City actually has an Eighteenth Dynasty loaf from Thebes that was buried more than thirty-four hundred years ago along with the Princess Meryet-Amum. The bread is disk-shaped and has a hole through its middle. Some of the pictured Egyptian breads look very much like the breads we make today, although the method of manufacture was distinctly different: it is believed that the Egyptians kneaded dough with their feet!

At first, the Egyptians milled barley and wheat with heavy grindstones and mixed the flour with water. Then they shaped the dough into the usual flat cakes and baked them in ovens that had been dug into the ground and lined with clay. As an interesting alternative (invented, perhaps, by someone who had no oven) they wrapped flat strips of dough around the outsides of earthen jugs and then built fires inside the jugs. Whatever the method of baking, the finished bread was always dense, heavy, and flat because it was unleavened.

But then the Egyptians made an important discovery. Although the Hebrews had long made their bread rise with fermented grain, it was the Egyptians who discovered that it wasn't the sour grain itself that made dough light, but rather the wild yeast plants that flourished in it. Some scholars say that the Egyptians learned to raise pure yeast from spores, whereas others believe that they simply learned they could leaven a new batch of dough with a piece of dough saved from the last baking—but whichever method they used, they revolutionized the art of baking bread. Not only did the breads rise uniformly and predictably, but the bakers of Egypt also developed new strains of wheat which could be ground into very fine flour, and they turned out truly fantastic loaves. So inspired were they by their light and airy dough that they began to blend grains together to make a variety of exciting and delicious new textures and flavors. In bursts of unprecedented culinary creativity they even baked breads that contained such exotic ingredients as honey, almonds, dates, figs, herbs, saffron, and cinnamon. Breads sweetened with honey and fruits and perfumed with spice! No one had ever dreamed of such food. These delicacies, though, were only for the rich; the poor got along, as they had before, with a primitive flat cake made of coarsely ground papyrus reeds (bulrush) and lotus root.

The history of bread takes us next, in a big leap, to ancient Greece during the Classical period where a form of barley bread was made. It did not figure importantly in the diet, however, since the Greeks more often made grains into pastes and porridges than into baked goods.

In ancient Rome, though, bread was once more in the forefront. It became so important that in a famous satire Juvenal wrote that the Romans needed only two things—*panem et circenses,* bread and circuses (entertainments).

There were at least sixty-two different kinds of Roman bread, both raised and flat. Bread was distributed free of charge to the needy as an early form of public welfare, and politicians gave it away when they campaigned.

During their first forays into North Africa the Romans had built a number of aqueducts which irrigated two thousand miles of coastland; later that land became extremely fertile and yielded enormous quantities of grain. Egypt had long been a great grain producer, and together these two sectors of Africa formed a bountiful breadbasket for the Roman Empire.

When the grain arrived in Rome, it was the miller who had to pound and clean it before he could even begin to grind. By the second century A.D. the miller had taken over the entire operation and become the baker, too. It may have been at this time that leavened bread was first made in Italy.

Public bakeries had become big business by the period of the early Empire, but even in those days businesses were subject to occasional setbacks. For example, during the first century A.D., all mills had to close because the Emperor Caligula had decided that his armies needed more draft animals, and he "conscripted" all the beasts that plodded in circles to turn the huge grindstones. Later, in the sixth century, the Goths invaded Rome and cut off the water that turned the many water wheels that were in use by that time.

But people baked bread no matter what happened. Accustomed

to a variety of "power failures" at the public bakeries, most Roman homes kept rotary or saddle querns (hand-operated mills) so that they could grind their own grain just as their ancestors had. The ruins of Pompeii revealed grain mills and ovens in many of the private homes.

Homemade bread was probably cheaper than "store-bought," and possibly people who were very particular felt that they could make a better loaf than they could purchase. We know that there was interest in and concern about bread quality, for Galen, the great Greek physician and medical writer who lived from about 130 to 200 A.D., told his readers:

Bread baked in the ashes is heavy and hard to digest because the baking is uneven. That which comes from a small oven or stove causes dyspepsia and is hard to digest. But bread made over a brazier or in a pan, owing to the admixture of oil, is easier to excrete, though steam from the drying makes it rather unwholesome. Bread baked in large ovens, however, excels in all good qualities, for it is well flavored, good for the stomach, easily digested, and very readily assimilated.

Although most of us tend to think of butter when we think of bread, butter was almost unknown in Greece or Rome. The common household fat was olive oil, but even this was not used on bread. According to the food historian Reay Tannahill in *Food in History,* both leavened and flat plain breads were probably eaten with meat or soaked in wine or milk; the flavored breads were considered meals in themselves and were generally taken with only a beverage.

The Romans introduced their fine breads to all corners of the Empire, and when the Romans lost their power and the Empire collapsed, the bread stayed on and became a staple of European diet during the Middle Ages. Peasant families commonly ate meals of bread and ale with a bit of salt pork or an onion as accompaniment. The bread was brown, made chiefly of rye, perhaps with some pea and barley flours added. In higher-class households, the bread was made of a mixture of rye and wheat.

From time to time, the grain crops were ruined by parasites and then monstrous famines swept the Continent. And there were other calamities, too. One of them occurred in 857 A.D., when a curious—and devastating—illness struck the population of the

Rhine Valley. Perfectly healthy people suddenly began to scream with excruciating stomach pains; a short time later they broke out in fiery rashes, became delirious, and died. They didn't know it, but the dread ailment came from bread that had been made with contaminated rye flour. Ergot is a fungus that attacks rye, and the affected grain contains twenty known poisons—among them, lysergic acid diethymide, better known as LSD. Europeans suffered from repeated outbreaks of ergotism; because afflicted people were driven mad by the unbearable skin rash, the disease was called "holy fire."

During the hundred years following 857, there were twenty major famines in Europe, and some of them lasted for several years at a time. But in spite of such enormous setbacks, the art of agriculture continued to advance, and as it did, bread grew ever more popular. It even became more than just a food.

In medieval Europe only the extremely wealthy had plates and drinking cups. No one had forks, and rich and poor alike ate with their fingers. The usual method of dining was to reach into a common bowl, lift out a piece of food, and drop it onto a *trencher*, a thick square of unleavened bread that was generally shared by two diners. The absorbent "plate" soaked up juices and gravy; when the meal was over, the very poor ate their trenchers, but those who were better off gave them to beggars or threw them to the dogs.

Trenchers remained in use for a long time after table utensils had become quite common, and in 1500 an anonymous author wrote the following rules of etiquette for children:

> *Lay a clean trencher before you, and when your pottage is brought, take your spoon and eat quietly; and do not leave your spoon in the dish, I pray you. Lay salt honestly on your trencher, for that is courtesy.*
>
> *Do not put the meat off your trencher into the dish, but get a voider and empty it into that.*
>
> *Do not play with the spoon, or your trencher, or your knife; but lead your life in cleanliness and honest manners.*
>
> *Heap not thy trencher with many morsels,*
> *And from blackness keep thy nails.*

In Britain, as on the Continent, bread became more and more important during the Middle Ages and became unquestionably established as the staple food of the land; in fact, by 1155, London bakers had formed a bakers' brotherhood, a sort of union.

In Continental Europe, however, there were bakers' guilds that were not for the benefit of the bakers at all, but rather were intended to protect the public. They were the means by which governments controlled and regulated baking. The rules were strict and the punishment for breaking them severe. In Austria, any baker who disobeyed the laws regulating the weight of each loaf, its cleanliness, and so forth, was fined, imprisoned, or flogged.

Strict measures weren't confined to Europe or even to such early times; in Turkey, during the eighteenth century, several bakers were hanged because their prices were too high, and in Turkey and Egypt, bakers who sold lightweight or dirty bread were nailed by an ear to their doorposts.

In Britain, a militant bread consumer with literary aspirations published a pamphlet in 1757. It sold for one shilling and sixpence, and its title page announced in a large scare headline: POISON DE-TECTED. With totally mystifying punctuation, the page continues:

or

Frightful Truths;

and

Alarming to the British Metropolis.

IN A

TREATISE ON BREAD:

and the

Abuses practiced in making that Food,

As occasioning the decrease and degeneracy of

the people; destroying infants; and producing

innumerable diseases.

Shewing also,

The virtues of GOOD BREAD, *and*

the manner of making it.

To which is added,

A CHARGE *to the confederacy of bakers, corn-dealers, farmers, and millers; concerning short weight, adulterations, and artificial scarcities; with easy methods to prevent all such abuses.*

BY MY FRIEND, *a Physician.*

By the time the good physician wrote his treatise, bread had long been established in the New World. It had come initially with the Spanish explorers, but Cortez had brought wheat to plant as well as the finished product, and one of his servants sowed the seeds in Mexico. It did well, and the first crop was harvested in 1530.

When the early New England colonists arrived, they too planted wheat they had brought from Europe. While they waited for it to mature, they learned from the Indians how to grind corn and make corn-meal bread.

The first wheat crops were ready in 1621, and as the colonies grew, each one built a community baking oven. In order to make bread each family had to do its own grinding, a time-consuming and laborious process. But in 1626 Peter Minuit, first governor of New Amsterdam, had a public mill built on Manhattan Island. Immediately, New York became the milling center of the colonies and remained so until 1750, when Philadelphia took over. By this time, the gristmill, powered by water or wind, had become a familiar sight in all the colonies, but in 1786 there was a monumental development: a flour mill powered by the exciting new steam engine ushered in a new era.

Though steam as a power source was revolutionary, all mills still ground with millstones. Larger, somewhat more sophisticated versions of the earliest grinding tool ever known, millstones were simply two flat stones that rubbed grain between their surfaces. They remained in use for nearly a hundred years more, until the middle of the nineteenth century.

It was at that time that a sensational new flour-making process was developed in Hungary. Hungarian flour was said to be the finest, lightest, whitest the world had ever seen. Word of this success was of special interest in what was then the northwestern sector of the United States, for though the area produced abundant wheat, it was harder than the variety that grew in warmer climates, and a large part of it was wasted when it was milled in gristmills. The new Hungarian process used rollers instead of grindstones, and it occurred to the governor of Minnesota that rollers might transform the problem wheat into an outstanding cash crop. He sent for a team of Hungarian engineers who came and set up a roller mill in Minneapolis; it was an instant success.

The hard wheat passed through a series of rollers that grew successively smaller in size; this system made it possible for the flour to be milled with a minimum of waste. Then the flour passed through sieves of increasing fineness, a process known as *bolting*. Bolted flour is light and airy, and when it is baked, it rises higher than coarser flour. Everyone wanted the new flour, and Minneapolis soon became a great milling center.

As the milling industry grew and spread, so did commercial bakeries. Virtually unknown until this time, "store" bread became so popular that by the beginning of World War I home bread-baking was becoming a thing of the past. From that time until now, commercial baking has been one of the giant industries of our nation; whole generations of Americans have never known any bread but the fluffy, white, spongy loaf that comes sliced and wrapped from gleaming machines, devoid of real goodness but filled with additives.

"Sanitary" bread marked a low point in the annals of food, but fortunately, around 1960, a new and quickly burgeoning interest in foods that were natural, wholesome, and homemade developed in the United States. There had always been a stubborn handful of home bakers; suddenly there was a great surge of bread-baking in the communes and among the back-to-the-land people, and from them, the idea spread all over the nation. Within ten years, homemade bread had stopped being a rarity and, in fact, was becoming commonplace again. And it wasn't only housewives who were baking bread this time; it was men, women who worked outside the home, boys, and girls. Americans knew a good thing when they tasted it. They also liked *doing* it.

Homemade bread does take some time, and so it may never totally displace the forty million commercial loaves that are still sold daily. But as more and more people experience the joy of baking, the word spreads; the kitchens of America are producing more loaves of bread than they have in more than fifty years—and the number increases every day.

2

A Loaf of Bread

A Jug of Wine, a Loaf of Bread—and Thou
Beside me singing in the Wilderness—

So spoke the Persian poet, Omar Khayyám, describing a personal vision of paradise. Surely the bread Omar had in mind was tender, crusty, crunchy, perhaps still warm from the oven and enveloped in delicious fragrance. Since the poet died in 1123 we can't be sure of the details, but one thing we can be absolutely certain of is that the immortalized bread didn't come from a supermarket.

It's easy to wax poetic about bread; no other food has been mentioned as often in literature. Bread is unique, too, in its importance in religious ceremonies from earliest times; the Christian sacrament of bread and wine put an "official" stamp upon the holy significance bread had had in many different rites that predated Christianity.

Perhaps bread was included in those early ceremonies because of its unmistakable aura of magic and mystery, the special quality that comes from the fact that bread dough—or at least the yeast in it—is alive. Like all living things, it is never completely predictable, and therein lies the enchantment—and for the baker, the challenge as well. No matter how carefully you follow the instructions, you can never make *exactly* the same bread twice.

Though we know that a baked mixture of flour and water is technically "bread," a *loaf* of bread is a bread that contains yeast or some other leavening agent. The so-called quick breads are raised with baking powder or soda (or both), and although they are easy to make and often delicious, they are not surrounded by any special mystique. Baking a quick bread is like baking a cake —pleasurable, worthwhile, predictable, routine. But ah, a yeast bread! Baking one is a life experience that no one should miss.

YEAST

Yeast, the magical ingredient, is actually a microscopic plant. It is dormant in its dry state, but as soon as you moisten and feed it, it comes to life. Yeast thrives on water and sugar—provided the temperature is right. It remains inactive if the temperature is too low; it dies if it gets too hot. Perhaps our need to care for yeast tenderly, to watch over it thoughtfully, to maintain the delicate balance of conditions necessary to keep it alive, creates our feeling of mystical relationship.

Yeast is not just another food, nor is it just another plant. It is a particular kind of plant cell that grows by putting out a bump on one side, a bud; as soon as the bud reaches the proper size, it breaks off and immediately becomes a new cell ready to put forth its own bud. Often three or four buds develop at once; the time it takes to grow a new generation is only about thirty minutes.

When yeasts are provided with liquid and carbohydrate, they feed on the latter, digest it, and bud. And in doing so, they give off alcohol and carbon dioxide, a gas. The carbon dioxide bubbles through the dough and puffs it full of tiny holes. It is these many small pockets filled with gas that make the dough rise until it has the texture of a sponge. When the bread is baked, the oven's heat kills the yeasts and drives off the alcohol. (Wine is made with yeast, too, but here the end result is quite different. Sugar and liquid are supplied by the grapes, and as the carbon dioxide is formed, it easily passes through the watery mixture into the air; it is the alcohol, here the desired end product, that remains.)

Though bread yeast can get all the food it needs from flour alone, it grows more quickly if it gets a head start from some form of concentrated sugar. That is why many bread recipes contain a small amount of sugar or honey, even if it is too little to impart any noticeable sweetness to the bread.

Yeast is the most exciting ingredient in bread because it is the one that is alive. And like most things that are alive and exciting, it's also rather temperamental—but not nearly as temperamental as it used to be. When yeast first became commercially available, it was sold only in paste form, either in bulk or as a "yeast cake." It had to be kept under refrigeration, and if it wasn't used promptly, the yeast—slowed down by the cold, but still needing some nourishment—soon died. That is why you will notice that most bread recipes (but not the ones in this book) tell you to "prove" the yeast before you do anything else. The term "prove" is used quite literally; the idea is to make sure that the yeast is alive. The yeast recipes in this book call for active dry yeast, a dry, granular yeast that is dormant. There is an expiration date on the package, and you should observe it, but as long as the package is unopened and the contents remain dry, this product has a very long life and does not need to be refrigerated.

Active dry yeast is commonly available in foil packets that weigh 7 grams, or ¼ ounce. It also comes in larger packets and in jars. If you are going to be baking bread regularly (and once you begin, you surely are), it's handier and cheaper to buy the larger size. Keep the yeast in the refrigerator after the package has been opened, and make sure that you keep it dry in a closely capped jar. Use 1 level tablespoon to equal 1 small packet.

Dry yeast becomes activated when it is mixed with liquid, and for quick growth, the liquid must be warm. The ideal temperature is between 110° and 115° F. At lower temperatures, yeast grows slowly and makes bread-baking a very lengthy procedure; at much higher temperatures than those recommended, yeast dies—so be careful. If you have a candy thermometer, use it the first time and stick your finger in the liquid to see what the right temperature feels like. If you don't have a suitable thermometer, use water that feels just about right for a baby's bath—not hot, just comfortably warm.

FLOUR

As soon as the yeast begins to get lively, it needs food, and though you may give it some sugar for a quick start, it will grow mainly on—and in—flour. There are many kinds of flour, and despite the fact that white flour makes the lightest cakes and pastries-that-melt-in-your-mouth, it makes the least interesting and the least nutritious bread. Whole-wheat flour, as its name implies, is made from the whole wheat berry, and is the natural, complete, basic bread flour. It has a rich wheaty taste and is the true "staff of life" because it is so rich in protein, vitamins, and minerals.

A single wheat berry, or grain of wheat, is made up of three parts. The *germ* is the seed that can grow into a new plant; it is our richest natural source of vitamin E. The outer hull of the berry is *bran.* It provides roughage, and only recently researchers have discovered that its inclusion in the diet may protect us against some serious diseases, including cancer of the colon. The largest part of the wheat berry is the *endosperm.* It is mainly starch and little else—and this is the part of the wheat from which white flour is made.

The minimal nutritional value of white flour is reduced even further when it is chemically bleached to make it whiter—and *only* bleached flour is used to make the bland, fluffy, wrapped bread that so many Americans are addicted to. Even though the law requires that such bread be "enriched" by the addition of a few vitamins, they don't begin to make up for the nutrients that were removed in the first place.

But the tide is beginning to turn. Commercial bakeries all over the nation report a greatly increased and increasing demand for whole-grain breads, and as a result, the industry has begun to market many new varieties of wholesome breads. Some of them are pretty good, too—but still not as good as the loaf you make at home.

You can make a good, dark, dense, chewy, hearty homemade

bread with the whole-wheat flour you buy in any market. But if you are a purist and want the best, you will have to look for *stone-ground* whole-wheat flour. This is made by the old-fashioned method of grinding, which is slower and less efficient than modern milling but does not subject the grain to high temperatures as rollers do. It loses fewer of its vitamins and minerals as a result and has a slightly different taste and texture. If you can purchase stone-ground flour easily, it is recommended, but it is not absolutely essential.

It seems important to note that nothing makes white bread except white flour; some homemade white breads are magnificent, and some of the time you are going to want to make them. You will also need white flour to make many breads that use both white and dark flour. When you shop, you will find that there are both bleached and *un*bleached white flours on the store shelf; buy the unbleached kind. Although it is minus the bran and germ of whole-wheat flour, it is also minus the chemicals of bleached flour, and has a better flavor—and is better for you.

The reason white flour is often mixed with whole-grain flour is that wheat flour is very rich in *gluten,* a protein that makes dough stretchy and elastic. Some flours, such as rye and soy, have so little gluten that the dough they make doesn't rise well. In order to use these flours successfully, we boost the gluten by adding some wheat flour—usually white—to the dough.

As dough is kneaded the gluten gets more and more stretchy. It finally becomes so elastic that when the yeast begins to send out its gas bubbles, the dough puffs up and the many small cells that hold the gas don't break. Well-kneaded dough has the consistency of bubble gum. Without gluten—or without yeast—bread would turn out like matzoh or crackers.

In addition to flours, whole grains and meals can be added to bread, too. Oats, corn meal, and wheat berries can be found in some of the recipes in this book.

THE OTHER INGREDIENTS

So far, we have discussed only the basic ingredients that were used (along with water) to make bread in earliest times, but modern breads usually contain a few more refinements. We add salt for flavor, and may add sweetener for the same purpose. Honey is called for in many of the recipes in this book, but you can substitute an equivalent amount of sugar if you want to. Molasses is used in some of the dark breads, and it has a very distinctive flavor; substituting sugar will make the bread taste quite different (and will lighten the color), so unless you particularly dislike molasses, do not make any change.

Fat is sometimes added to bread to make it richer, softer, and to make it keep better. You can always substitute melted butter or margarine if you prefer, but oil is called for in most of the recipes (except in the dessert breads). It is easier to use since you don't have to melt it, and, unlike butter, it is not high in cholesterol. The best oils are safflower, soy, and corn, but you can use any light cooking oil except olive—unless the recipe specifically calls for olive oil.

Some breads contain milk, which makes a fine texture and adds nutrients. For the sake of convenience, all the yeast recipes in this book call for powdered dry skim milk. In order to make bread with regular milk, you have to scald the milk and then wait for it to cool to lukewarm (to avoid killing the yeast). When you use dry milk you don't have to scald it because that has already been done in its preparation. You can mix it with water that is exactly the right temperature to begin with and not waste time waiting for it to cool. (And you don't have to wash an extra pot!)

There are all sorts of other things you can put into bread: eggs for richness and a "cakier" texture, spices, herbs, fruits, fruit juice, vegetables, nuts, flavorings of every kind; these are all embellishments and need no explanation other than that they taste good.

If you have never baked bread before, you have a great new experience to look forward to—and don't be anxious about it. Baking bread is easy! Even if your first loaf doesn't look exactly like the picture in the book (it might look better), it's almost impossible to have a failure. Bread is always different, but it's almost always good. It's *hard* to ruin bread, and without doubt, that's one of the secrets of its long-lasting success. It's difficult even to imagine all the different kinds of people who baked different kinds of breads under all sorts of conditions over thousands and thousands of years. If they could do it, so can you.

So plunge in. Put your hands into warm, soft dough. Feel it

change, come alive, as you work it. See it turn smooth and satiny as you coax it into form. Feed the yeasts so that they prosper and multiply until they make your dough light as down. Put the loaves into the oven and fill the kitchen and the house with magnificent, mouth-watering fragrance. Cut your bread and hand a hot and crumbly slice to someone you love. Bake bread and fill your heart with joy.

3

How to Do It

In the last chapter we made the flat claim that it's easy to bake bread. Here are some of the things that *make* it easy.

You hardly ever have to measure anything very carefully.

You never have to sift anything.

You can let yeast dough sit around for a long time and nothing terrible happens to it.

You can slam the oven door and the bread won't fall.

With that much latitude it isn't easy to make mistakes—but even if you do, you can nearly always correct them.

EQUIPMENT

To begin, you will need a measuring cup, and though you can get along with a 1-cup size, it's handy to have a 2-cup, or a 4-cup size as well. A wooden spoon is best for mixing, and you'll need a teaspoon and a tablespoon for measuring, some baking pans, and mixing bowls.

First, the pans. Since homemade bread seems to get eaten very fast, it doesn't pay to make a single loaf. All the recipes that follow (except some for sweet or fancy breads) make two loaves; therefore, you will need two pans. A standard- or large-size bread pan is roughly 9 × 5 inches, a medium one about 8 × 4 inches. There are smaller pans in a variety of sizes. U-shaped French-bread pans come in many sizes, too, and they are generally attached in pairs, like Siamese twins.

If you don't have bread pans and are planning to buy some, you will find many kinds to choose from. The very best ones are made of extremely heavy black steel (called bakers' steel). They hold the heat and develop a marvelous bread crust, but they are quite expensive and are in the luxury class.

More moderate in price, and completely satisfactory in every way, are pans coated with Teflon or silicone. If you use these, grease them in spite of their nonstick coatings, and you will never have to worry about getting your bread out of the pan in one piece.

Plain, ordinary loaf pans made of aluminum or other metal, or glass, will do perfectly well, too. If you use glass pans, you have to remember to lower the oven temperature in every recipe by 25°F.

If you don't want to bother with pans at all, bake your bread in any ovenproof container that isn't smaller at the top than it is at the bottom. Soufflé dishes, casseroles, small roasters, even clay flowerpots are all usable. (Size doesn't matter as long as you don't fill any container much more than halfway when you put in the dough.) To bake in a clay flowerpot, make sure it's clean (good bread may be earthy, but it isn't supposed to *taste* like earth), put a circle of foil in the bottom to cover the hole, and when you grease the pot, grease the foil, too.

Coffee cans, either 1- or 2-pound size, make very attractive breads. Even if you have regular pans, you will enjoy using these (as well as casseroles and the like) for variation. Because of the deep cylindrical shape and the ridges in a coffee can, it is often hard to get bread out of it. To make sure that you have no problem, grease the can well, then sprinkle in a little corn meal and tilt the can so that the meal sticks to the bottom and sides. This makes a nice crust, too. It is a good trick to use with *any* kind of container you have doubts about or whenever your dough is a sticky one.

Round breads can be baked in cake pans, and both round and long shapes can be placed on flat baking sheets as long as the dough is stiff enough to hold its shape. Use cookie pans, the bottom part of a broiler pan, or a large roasting pan.

Now for the bowls. All standard bread recipes tell you to mix the dough in a bowl and then turn it out on a floured board to knead—but I have always found that cleaning that awful board is the only part of baking that I really dislike. A board large enough to work on is usually too large to fit into the sink conveniently and it manages, sneakily, to dump puddles of water all over the floor while I'm scrubbing away at the stuck dough and the flour-and-water paste. If I use a small board, the floor winds up covered with flour. It always seemed like a losing game; so now I don't use a board at all; I mix—and knead—my bread in a plastic dishpan.

A round dishpan has sides just high enough to keep the flour and dough inside but low enough for your arms to reach over; it has a large flat bottom that is perfect for kneading; the plastic holds the heat well so that the dough stays warm, and the pan is just the right size to sit in the sink and soak itself clean. If you don't have a plastic dishpan, buy one. It requires only a small investment and is worth it many times over. (If you prefer a classical approach—or are just plain stubborn—go ahead and use a board.)

TECHNIQUE

You will notice that almost all the yeast-bread recipes in this book call for a variable amount of flour, such as 4 to 6 cups. That is because there is a tremendous difference in flours; they vary from brand to brand, and even a given brand may vary from batch to batch because it was made with different wheat. In addition, dough is strongly affected by temperature and humidity. The same recipe will require different amounts of flour on hot, humid days and on cold, dry days. Occasionally, you may have to use even more than the maximum amount mentioned in the recipe. It's perfectly all right to do so as long as you do it slowly. You can always add more flour but you can't take any out, so be very careful. Add the minimum amount of flour first, then add a little more at a time until you can handle the dough.

Dough is "ready to handle" when you can pick it up. At first, it should be like soft clay, very sticky but not so wet that it sags through your fingers when you pick up a handful. To find out if you can handle it, pick it up and see. As soon as it's ready, stop adding flour and begin to knead.

There is more than one way to knead, and with a little practice you will develop your own style. You can knead with one hand and switch to the other when the first one gets tired, or you can knead with both hands at once. Do whatever feels comfortable and work on a surface that is low enough for you to put your body weight behind your arms. Unless you are extremely tall you will find kitchen counters too high for kneading, so try the table.

If you are kneading right in your dishpan (and we hope you are), sprinkle a small amount of flour over the top of the dough, sprinkle a little more on your hands, scoop the dough together and turn it over. (If it's impossible to turn over, it needs more flour.) Now sprinkle a little more flour over the top and press down and away from your body with the heel of your hand(s). If you are using a board, dust it with flour before you put the dough on it and then proceed in exactly the same way.

After a few strokes, fold the dough over from back to front and knead some more. When you pick up the back edge to fold it forward, sprinkle a tiny bit of flour on the exposed part of the pan or board if the dough sticks to it. After each few folds and kneads, turn the lump of dough about a quarter of the way around.

At first, the term "fold" may not have much meaning. Even though you can bend the mass over, it hardly makes a neat fold, but as you keep working and the gluten begins to develop, the dough will begin to hold its shape nicely. It will even stop sticking in huge globs to your fingers. If this doesn't happen within a few minutes, shake in a little more flour. In a very short time you will get the "feel" of when the dough is just right.

Continue to knead, fold, and turn for anywhere from four to ten minutes—or longer if the recipe calls for it. The dough will become so elastic and springy that it will begin to feel like a soft rubber ball. When you press it, it fights back. It also develops a smooth, satiny look and may have little blisters on its surface. Now you can easily form the dough into a ball and pick up the whole thing in one hand and it will hold its shape. At this point, it is ready for the first rising.

If you are using the dishpan method, you can let the dough rise in the same pan. You do not have to wash the pan, but do dump out any excess flour or scraps of dry dough that may be lurking on the bottom. Pick up the dough and pour a little oil (about a teaspoonful) into the pan and spread it around. Put the dough down on it, then turn the dough over so that the oily side is up. Cover it with plastic wrap or a clean dish towel and put it in a warm place so that the yeast will grow quickly and make the dough rise.

Unless it is being used for something else, the oven is the best place. If you have a gas oven with a pilot light, you are in luck, because when the oven is turned off the pilot light provides a temperature that is just about perfect. If you have no pilot light, try leaving the electric light bulb on. And if you don't have a bulb, set a pan of very hot water in the bottom of the oven. The heavy insulation of the oven walls will keep in the heat for a long time.

If you can't tie up the oven, you will have to find another warm spot (except in very hot weather). Since heat rises, a high shelf in a kitchen cupboard is often much warmer than a counter top. Do not put the dough over a pilot light or on the radiator since too much heat will kill the yeast.

Recipes usually tell you to let the dough rise until it has "doubled in bulk." It's a little hard to tell when the dough looks like twice as much as you started with, but when you think it is about right, stick a finger into it. If you make a hole as deep as your first finger joint and the hole remains when you take your finger out, the dough has risen enough.

The next step is known as "punching down." The dough has risen because it is full of gas bubbles, and punching it is like puncturing a balloon; the gas escapes and the dough deflates. After it flattens, fold it over a few times and press it down with the palms of your hands to force out any gas that is left.

Now you are ready to shape the dough into loaves. To fit a loaf pan, press the dough into a rectangle (in the dishpan or on the table) a little longer than the pan. Starting with one of the long sides, roll the dough tightly and pinch the seam together. Turn it over so that the seam is on the bottom and tuck the ends under neatly. Don't worry if the loaf is smaller than the pan because it has to rise again, and when it does, it will fill up the leftover space.

To make a round or oval loaf, slap the dough hard on the tabletop, cupping your hands around it each time to mold it. For a long bread, like a French or Italian loaf, proceed as for a loaf-pan bread, only make a much longer, narrower rectangle. If you are going to bake your bread on a flat pan or baking sheet, you can make it any shape you want. To bake in a coffee can or other unorthodox container, just form the dough into roughly the same shape as the container and drop it in.

You can vary basic shapes and make them look different: when you make a round bread (in a casserole or cake pan) save a small piece of dough when you make the big round, then make a small round and set it on top, right in the center. When you make a long bread, turn it into a spiral by giving it a twist. Make braided breads by dividing the dough into three strands, rolling them with your hands into ropes, and braiding them together. You can make patterned breads by baking them in special molds such as bundt pans.

Whenever you make a very large loaf, it is a good idea to cut some slits in it to let the steam escape. Use a sharp knife or a single-edge razor blade and make the cuts quite deep. For a long loaf, make three or four diagonal slits crosswise, or one long slit down the center. For round loaves, make several diagonal slits or a cross.

When the loaves have been prepared, it is time for the second rising. Cover the pans as before and put them back in the warm rising place. The second rising usually takes only half as long as the first one.

When you put the pans into the oven, put them on a fairly low shelf so that the top of the bread will be approximately in the center of the oven. Don't let the pans touch each other and don't let them touch the sides of the oven.

Unless otherwise specified, the oven should be preheated (with the pans out of it, of course; a short wait on the counter won't do the dough any harm). Although the heat kills the yeast, there is some delay before the heat penetrates to the center of the loaf, so you can expect some further rising during the first few minutes of baking even though the oven is hot.

To make a very crisp crust, brush the tops of the loaves with cold water (use either a pastry brush or your fingers) just before baking. You can repeat the cold-water treatment once or twice more during the baking period if you want to. A pan of hot water set in the bottom of the oven to steam makes a very crusty bread, too. If you prefer soft crust, brush the tops of the loaves with butter or oil before baking.

Use a timer for baking, but only as an approximate guide; to test bread for doneness, turn it out of the pan and rap it on the bottom with your knuckles. It should make a hollow sound. If it doesn't, put it back for a few minutes and try again. If the bottom isn't brown enough, take the bread out of the pan and put it directly on the oven rack.

As soon as bread is removed from the oven it should be turned out of the pan and placed, right side up or on its side, on a wire rack to cool. If you leave hot bread on a solid surface, the bottom will get soggy from steam.

All the breads freeze well but you have to let them cool *thoroughly* before you seal them in plastic bags or aluminum foil. To use frozen bread, let it thaw, then heat it in a moderate oven for 10 to 15 minutes.

You can cut any recipe in half by using half of each ingredient —with one exception: if the original directions call for only one packet or one tablespoon of yeast, use it all even though you are halving everything else. If the directions call for *two* or more packets of yeast, cut the amount in half.

If you live at a high altitude (over 3000 feet) you will have to make some adjustments in leavening. Because of the lower air pressure, the carbon dioxide gas will rise more than it does at sea level, and it may stretch the dough too much and make a coarse-textured bread. You can either use about one-fourth less yeast, or let the dough rise twice instead of once before shaping the loaves, punching it down each time. For quick breads, reduce the baking powder or baking soda by one-fourth.

That's all you really have to know, but a list of helpful hints and emergency procedures follows.

MISCELLANEOUS HINTS

Measurements for yeast breads never have to be exact, as they do for cakes. Make a reasonable effort to be accurate, but do not bother to level off a cupful of flour with a spatula. Since large quantities of flour are often used, it saves time (and prevents your losing count) to use a large measuring cup. Just dip it into the canister or sack.

Never sift flour for yeast bread. Although most cookbooks require sifted flour for quick breads, this one does not. If you want to sift, go ahead, but I have never been able to perceive that it made any difference.

So that you can judge how much flour to buy, 1 pound equals about 3¾ cups.

Before kneading, scrub your hands and nails with a hand brush and remove your rings. You will find the brush useful after kneading, too.

For glazed, crispy top crust, instead of brushing the loaves with cold water before baking, use a slightly beaten egg white mixed with 1 tablespoon of cold water. Repeat during baking.

For very, very soft crust, brush the tops of the loaves with butter or oil before baking and repeat as soon as they are removed from the oven. Wrap them in plastic wrap while they are still slightly warm.

To store dough: Since all bread is best when freshly baked, you may want to mix a batch of dough and bake only part of it. Cover the remainder with plastic wrap (or put it in a plastic bag) and store it in the refrigerator. You can keep it for several days. It may continue to rise a very little bit even at refrigerator temperature, so keep an eye on it. If it appears to grow, punch it down, then store it again. Dough will keep for several weeks in the freezer. Thaw it, then pick up the procedure wherever you left off.

To store bread: Bread gets stale because it loses its moisture, and contrary to what most people think, it does that faster in the refrigerator than it does at room temperature. Therefore, the best place to keep baked bread is in a breadbox or plastic bag at room temperature in the kitchen. Bread does, however, get moldy quickly in warm, humid weather, so under those conditions you have no choice but to refrigerate it. The best plan is always to keep out just enough for immediate use and freeze the rest.

Breads made with oil or butter stay fresh longer than those made without fat.

Although it is a great temptation to cut bread as soon as it comes out of the oven, most breads cut and taste better if you let them cool somewhat first.

You can always substitute butter or margarine for oil if you prefer. Melt it first and let it cool to lukewarm. Measure it *after* it is melted.

You can always substitute honey, molasses, white or brown sugar for each other, although they have different flavors. They also have somewhat different sweetening power, but for bread recipes in which only small quantities are used, it doesn't really matter. If you use honey or molasses instead of sugar, you might have to use a little extra flour—but the amount of flour is variable anyway.

You can greatly increase the protein value of white flour if you do the following: Every time you measure 1 cup of flour, put 1 tablespoon each of soy flour, wheat germ, and nonfat dry milk powder into the cup first, then add the flour. This mixture is called Cornell flour after the university where it was developed by Dr. Clive M. McCay and his coworkers.

You can add chopped nuts, cheese, raisins, currants, a little leftover cooked cereal or rice, a bit of mashed potato, herbs, or whatever, to almost any bread dough when you feel experimental; instead of water you can use fruit juice or water from cooked vegetables for special flavors.

If dough rises either too much or too fast, the bread will have a poor texture.

No matter what you do, the odds are against your bread coming out exactly the same way twice; that's part of the excitement. Don't reject your bread just because it's different. Although it may not be precisely what you expected, it's probably very good—and just possibly even *better* than you expected.

EMERGENCY PROCEDURES AND DIAGNOSES

If you are interrupted in the middle of baking yeast bread, don't worry about it. If the interruption is a phone call, just cover the dough to keep it from drying out—and don't talk too long. If someone invites you to play two sets of tennis while the dough is rising, punch it down, cover it with plastic wrap, and put it in the refrigerator until you get back. If someone invites you to Paris for a month, put the dough in the freezer. In all cases, you will be able to pick up just where you left off when you get back. (These rules do *not* apply to quick breads, which can be set aside before the leavening has been added but *must* be baked promptly after it has.)

If you forget to keep an eye on the dough while it's rising (even if it's in the pans) and it much more than doubles its bulk, punch it down and let it rise again. But this time do watch it; it rises much faster the second time. Actually, a number of risings makes a fine texture, so you might even want to do it that way on purpose some of the time.

If your dough doesn't rise at all, either the yeast was dead when you started or you killed it with too much heat. The only thing you can do is begin again. Test the yeast by putting a tablespoonful into ¼ cup of warm water with a few grains of sugar. If the mixture becomes foamy in 5 to 10 minutes, your yeast is alive and well and you can use it—and this time, make certain that the water is only lukewarm. If the yeast remains inactive, discard it and buy a fresh supply.

If your bread has lumps in it, you didn't mix the dough thoroughly. Next time, be sure to beat in part of the flour before adding the last few cups, and always scrape the sides and bottom of the bowl well. If you find any dry scraps of dough clinging to the bowl or board, remember to throw them away instead of trying to work them in.

If your bread is pale and damp, you didn't bake it long enough. Put it back in the oven and bake it for another 15 to 20 minutes —even if you have cut it.

If the bread is soggy, you might have used too much liquid—or, to put it another way, not enough flour. Bread also becomes soggy if it's put into airtight containers before it is thoroughly cool.

If the bread starts to get very brown but still has a lot of baking time left, lay a piece of aluminum foil over the top. If your oven browns unevenly (as most do) shift the pans around in the middle of the baking period. Bread does not fall as cakes do, so it's all right to move it.

If your bread splits along the side while it's baking—I can't tell you why it does. It's a thing that just seems to happen sometimes; it happens to everyone and no one knows why, so just take it in stride. The bread tastes good anyway.

Now that you are prepared for just about everything, it's time to bake bread.

A NOTE ON MEASUREMENTS AND SIZES

All metric-English conversions have been made with ordinary kitchen measuring cups and not laboratory graduates in mind. *The equivalents are based on a system that makes a liter and a quart identical—as, of course, they are not.* However, for our purposes, they are quite close enough, so you can follow the directions in either system and they will work.

Numbers have been rounded off for convenience, so that 9 inches in the English system becomes 23 centimeters instead of 228.6 millimeters.

Teaspoons and tablespoons remain plain old-fashioned American teaspoons and tablespoons; you do not have to use special measuring spoons unless you choose to.

Pan sizes vary with manufacturers, and all sizes given are approximate—which is good enough. When numerical sizes are not given, use the following guide:

Large (or standard) loaf pans	23 × 13 cm. or 9 × 5 in.
Medium loaf pans	20 × 10 cm. or 8 × 4 in.
Small loaf pans	anything smaller than medium

Because bread doughs vary widely in volume, it is not practical to be absolutely precise about pan or other container sizes; rely on your eye—and common sense.

The Recipes

WHITE—OR MOSTLY WHITE— BREADS

BASIC WHITE BREAD

This bread is not called basic because it is the simplest kind of bread; as you know, bread that is really basic in that sense would be made only of flour and water, and a slightly more sophisticated version might contain salt. This bread has all those "basics," but in addition it contains yeast for leavening, sugar for flavor, fat for richness, and milk (instead of plain water) for texture. It is called basic because it can be used as a basis for many fancier breads. It is also the kind of bread that most Americans think of as a good, plain, basic, homemade loaf. It keeps well and can be used for any purpose, including sandwiches or toast. When it gets stale it makes fine bread crumbs.

The method of making this bread is basic, too, and once it is mastered, it provides guidelines for all other kinds of bread recipes. For example, when a recipe says that a particular dough tends to be sticky, that means it is stickier than basic dough. When the recipe says a dough takes longer to rise, that means it takes longer than basic dough does.

This is certainly not the only possible way to make bread, but it is a good standard method that will serve you well. Once you have learned it, you can consider yourself a bona fide bread-baker; you will be able to follow any recipe at all and even improvise to create your own variations.

	1 tablespoon (1 packet) active dry yeast
	1 tablespoon sugar
160 milliliters	**⅔ cup nonfat dry milk powder**
½ liter	**2 cups warm water (43–46°C, 110–115°F)**
	1 tablespoon salt
	3 tablespoons oil
1¼–1½ liters	**5–6 cups unbleached white flour**

1*   Put the yeast, sugar, milk powder, and warm water into a dish-pan or a large bowl. (For the sake of brevity and convenience—and because "dishpan" sounds so silly—we will, from this time on, say "bowl." But *you*'ll know it's a dishpan, won't you?) Stir with a wooden spoon, then add the salt, oil, and 3 cups of flour.

2   Beat well with the spoon for about 2 minutes. You can use an electric mixer if you prefer.

Add 2 cups more of flour, then measure 1 more cup and set it aside. That's so that you can add more flour later if necessary without making too much of a mess with your doughy hands. Speaking of doughy hands, this is a good time to put a plastic bag within easy reach so that you can slip your hand into it in case the phone rings; it almost always does.

3   Plunge your hand into the bowl and mix and squeeze until all the flour disappears. If the dough is so wet that you can't pick up a part of it, add a little more flour. As soon as you can handle the

4   dough, begin to knead. Sprinkle it with a light dusting of flour and dust a little under the dough, too. Dip your fingers into the flour cup whenever you need to.

At first the dough will be very sticky and will cling to all your

*These numbers refer to illustrations on pages 36-37.

fingers in big globs. But after a few minutes it will begin to stick to itself instead of to you and start to feel smooth. If it remains hopelessly sticky, you need more flour, but the trick is to use *just* enough and not too much.

Keep folding the dough over and pressing down and away with   5
the heel of your hand or hands. After every few strokes, turn the   6
lump of dough a little bit, fold, and knead some more.   7

When the dough begins to feel very smooth and bouncy and has a silky sheen, you can stop. It usually takes from 8 to 10 minutes to reach this stage, but since there are variations in flours, temperature, and humidity (as well as kneaders), readiness should not be judged by the clock.

Now it's time to cover the dough and put it in a warm place to double in bulk. Spread a little oil in the bottom of the same bowl you used for mixing, form the dough into a roundish lump, put   8
it into the bowl, and then turn it over. Put a piece of plastic wrap   9
or a towel over the top of the bowl and put it into the oven—or wherever your favorite warm rising place is—and go do something else for a while. Depending on conditions, you will have anywhere from 40 minutes to an hour, or an hour and a half, or even more in which to do it.

When the dough has doubled in bulk (a fingertip poked into the   10
dough leaves a hole), punch it down until it is completely deflated.   11
Give it a few extra kneads just to make sure.

Thoroughly grease (with oil or butter) two bread pans, each about 9 × 5 inches. Form the dough into a neat round and cut it   12
in half with a sharp knife. Pat each half into a rectangle just a little longer than the bread pans, then roll it up tightly starting at one   13
of the long sides. Pinch the seam together, turn the rolled dough over so that the seam is on the bottom, then tuck the ends under   14
neatly to make tidy loaves. Put each one into a prepared pan, cover   15
the pans with plastic wrap or a towel and put them back in the warm place to double in bulk again. This time it will take only   16
about half as long. When the loaves have risen enough, they will just about reach the tops of the pans.

Preheat the oven to 400°F and brush the tops of the loaves with   (17)
cold water. This makes a good crusty crust. If you prefer a soft   18
crust, omit this step and spread a little butter or oil on top instead. Repeat when the bread comes out of the oven.

Bake the bread for 35 minutes and then test it for doneness. In addition to looking well browned, it should have a hollow sound

19   when you turn it out of the pan and rap it on the bottom with your knuckle. If it isn't done, put it back—with or without the pans.

20   As soon as the bread is finished, remove it from the pans and set it on wire racks to cool. If you don't have wire racks, put each loaf sideways across the top of its baking pan so that air can circulate freely under it.

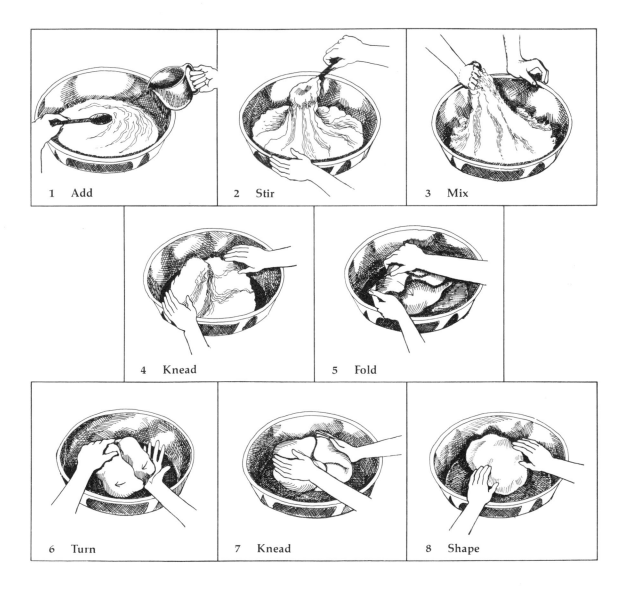

1   Add   2   Stir   3   Mix

4   Knead   5   Fold

6   Turn   7   Knead   8   Shape

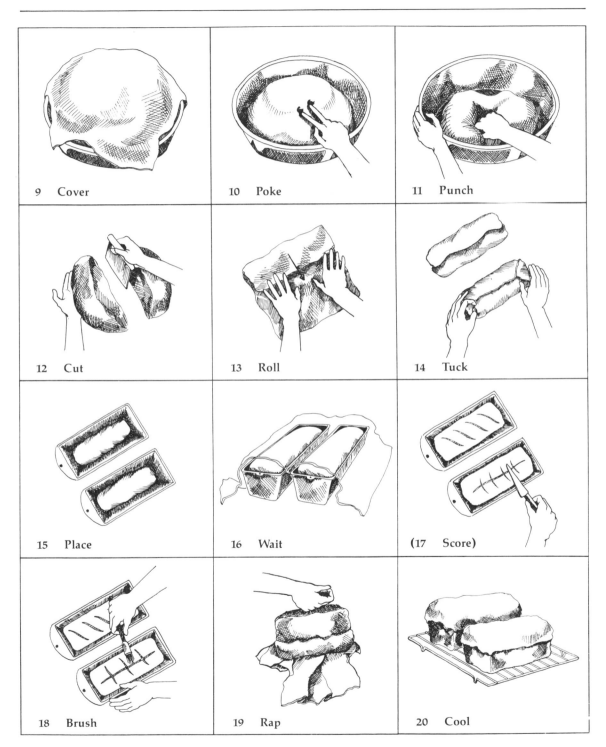

9 Cover

10 Poke

11 Punch

12 Cut

13 Roll

14 Tuck

15 Place

16 Wait

(17 Score)

18 Brush

19 Rap

20 Cool

🌿 *VARIATIONS* 🌿

All additions to the basic white-bread recipe should be made just before the dough is kneaded; if you make a *late* decision, knead in the extra ingredients just before you shape the loaves.

DILL BREAD

Add 2 tablespoons dried dill weed or 4 tablespoons of fresh, chopped dill.

MIXED HERB BREAD

Add 1 teaspoon each of dried basil, thyme, and oregano. You can also use 3 teaspoons of any one herb if you prefer.

ORANGE NUT BREAD

Omit the milk powder and warm water from the basic recipe and substitute 2 cups of lukewarm orange juice. Add 1 cup of seedless raisins or currants and ½ cup of chopped walnuts or pecans.

LIGHT RYE BREAD

Substitute 2 cups of rye flour for 2 cups of white flour.

CINNAMON RAISIN BREAD

Add 1 cup of seedless raisins and 2 teaspoons of cinnamon. If you want the bread to be slightly sweet, increase the amount of sugar to ¼ cup.

CHEESE BREAD

Omit the sugar and add 1 extra tablespoon of oil (a total of 4) and 1 cup of grated or shredded Cheddar or Gruyère cheese. You can also use all or part Parmesan. Bake Cheese Bread at 375°F and check it for doneness after 30 minutes.

LIGHT WHEAT-GERM BREAD

Add 1 cup of wheat germ *before* you add the flour.

This is a very simple white bread, but an attractive one. It has a good texture and a crisp crust. Its large slices make it particularly suitable for open-face sandwiches or really hefty closed ones.

You can copy the shape for any kind of bread at all.

ENGLISH COTTAGE BREAD

	2 tablespoons (2 packets) active dry yeast
½ liter	**2 cups warm water (43–46°C, 110–115°F)**
	2 teaspoons salt
1½–1¾ liters	**6–7 cups unbleached white flour**

Put the yeast and water into a large bowl and add the salt and 4 cups of flour. Beat well with a wooden spoon. Add 2 more cups of flour and begin to knead. Add more flour as necessary to make a firm, workable dough. Knead until it becomes smooth and elastic, for 5 to 7 minutes.

Grease the bottom of the bowl; put in the dough and then turn it over so that the greased side is up. Put it in a warm place to double in bulk.

When the dough is ready, punch it down and cut it in half; cut each half into two unequal parts—about two-thirds and one-third. Form the larger one into a very slightly flattened ball and put

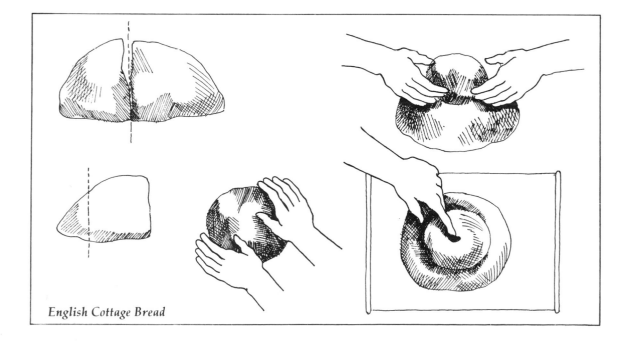

English Cottage Bread

it on a greased baking sheet. Form the smaller portion into another slightly flattened ball and set it on top of the larger one. Now stick your finger in flour and push it all the way through the center of both balls. Repeat with the rest of the dough to make a second loaf.

Cover the loaves and put them in a warm place to rise until they have doubled in bulk. Put them into an oven that has been pre-heated to 400°F; after 30 minutes, reduce the heat to 375°F and bake for about 20 minutes more, until the loaves are very brown.

FRENCH BREAD

The term "French bread," when it appears in a recipe intended for home use, is something of an exaggeration; it would be more accurate to say "French-style," or "Italian-style," or even just "Mediterranean-style bread." Real French bakery bread, that most superb of crusty breads that we buy in stores or eat in restaurants, is almost impossible to duplicate in a home kitchen. Among other differences, the ovens that turn out French bread professionally have heat coming from all sides, not just from the bottom as home ovens do.

Authentic or not, this is a perfect bread to serve at any time, but it is especially suitable for French or Italian meals since it is so handy for mopping up sauce or gravy. It is at its best when it is fresh from the oven, and in Europe it is customary to buy a fresh loaf for every meal. All over France one can see long, long loaves of bread sticking out of string bags, tied to the backs of bicycles, or clutched in the arms of children not much taller than the bread.

While very long loaves are convincingly French, your oven isn't, so you will have to make your bread to fit your oven-size baking pan. This recipe will make four very thin long loaves, two large round ones, or two medium-length loaves plus one round. If you have a pair of French-bread pans, use them and make a round loaf in a cake tin or a casserole. If you don't have the special pans, make all the loaves, of whichever shape you choose, on a baking sheet.

Since French bread does not keep at all well, freeze any that you do not plan to eat the first day. Follow the directions for freezing in Chapter 3.

There are many versions of French-bread recipes, and this is one that is fairly quick and easy to make. It should be kneaded for a

long time in order to achieve the proper texture, but you can
minimize your labor by replacing some of the kneading with beating. If you have an electric mixer, this is the time to use it.

	2 tablespoons (2 packets) active dry yeast
¾ liter	**3 cups warm water (43–46°C, 110–115°F)**
	1½ tablespoons salt
about 2 liters	**about 8 cups unbleached white flour**
	oil
	corn meal
	1 egg white mixed with 1 tablespoon cold water

Mix the yeast, water, salt, and 3 cups of flour in a large bowl.
Beat by hand or at medium speed with an electric mixer for 2
minutes. Add another 2 cups of flour and beat for 2 more minutes.
Now add 2 cups of flour and put about half as much into the
measuring cup while your hands are still clean.

Mix the dough with your hand until it is well blended, and add
more flour from the cup if necessary until the dough is stiff enough
to knead and handle easily. Knead for 8 to 10 minutes. The dough
must be perfectly smooth and very bouncy.

Grease the bowl, put in the dough and turn it over. Cover it and
put it in a warm place to rise until it has doubled in bulk.

Punch down the dough and cut it into two, three, or four parts,
depending on how many loaves you want to make. To form a long
loaf, flatten the dough into a rectangle about three-fourths the
length of your baking sheet. Starting with a long side, roll up the
dough tightly, then tuck under the ends.

If you are going to bake your bread on a baking sheet, do not
grease it but sprinkle it with a light covering of corn meal. If you
use French-bread pans, round pans, or casseroles, oil them first and
then sprinkle them with corn meal. Turn them upside down to
shake out the excess meal.

Put loaves on a baking sheet at some distance from each other
so that they will have room to expand. Cover the loaves, put them

in a warm place, and let them rise for 30 minutes. Make several diagonal slashes across the top of each loaf with a sharp knife or a razor blade, and brush the loaves with egg-white-and-water mixture. It's best to use a pastry brush (or a feather), but if you don't have one, do it very gently with your fingers.

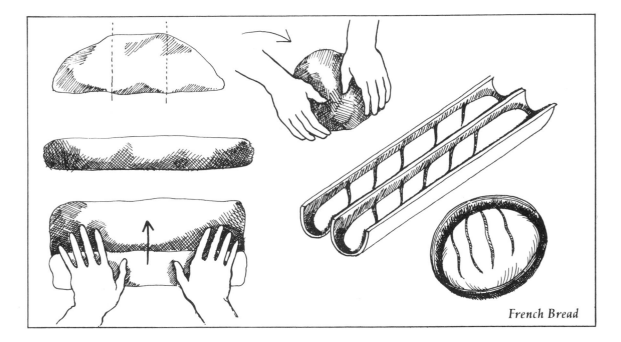

French Bread

Put the loaves into a cold oven and set a pan of very hot water in the bottom. Turn on the oven to 400°F. Bake the bread for 35 to 40 minutes, until it is nicely browned and sounds hollow when you tap it on the bottom. Cool it on racks—or eat it hot.

GREEN BREAD

This bread isn't *really* green—it takes its name from its profusion of finely chopped green herbs. It's a tangy, tasty bread, and an unusually attractive one.

If you have an herb garden, use fresh herbs instead of dried ones, but be sure to double the quantity. You can experiment with flavor changes by substituting dill or rosemary for the tarragon.

	2 tablespoons (2 packets) active dry yeast
½ liter	2 cups warm water (43–46°C, 110–115°F)
	4 tablespoons honey
1½–1¾ liters	7–8 cups unbleached white flour
	1½ tablespoons salt
	4 tablespoons oil
	3 eggs
	1 teaspoon dried basil
	1 teaspoon dried tarragon
120 milliliters	½ cup finely chopped fresh parsley
	pinch (about ¼ teaspoon) of cinnamon
	1 egg white mixed with 1 tablespoon cold water

Put the yeast, warm water, and honey into a large bowl. Add 3 cups of flour and beat well with a wooden spoon until the batter is perfectly smooth. Cover the bowl and put it in a warm place to rise until the sponge has doubled in bulk.

Stir, then with the wooden spoon beat in the salt, oil, eggs, basil, tarragon (rub the dried herbs between your fingers to powder them), and parsley. Add the cinnamon and most of the remaining flour.

Begin to knead, and add more flour if necessary to keep the dough from sticking. Knead for about 10 minutes, or until the dough is shiny and springy. Put it in an oiled bowl, turn it over, cover it with a damp towel, and let it rise in a warm place until it has doubled in bulk. Punch it down and let it rise a second time.

Punch the dough down again and cut it in half. Cut a lump the size of your fist off each half and set the lumps aside.

Butter a baking sheet and form the large pieces of dough into two balls. Put them on the baking sheet at a good distance from each other. Form the small pieces of dough into balls and place one on top of each large ball. Cover the loaves and let them rise until they have doubled in bulk.

Heat the oven to 375°F. Brush the loaves with the egg-white

glaze and bake them for about 35 minutes, or until the bread is as brown as old mahogany and sounds hollow when rapped. Remove from baking sheet and cool on racks.

TOMATO BASIL BREAD

This is a most unlikely-looking bread; it's salmon pink flecked with tiny bits of green. The shiny top crust looks pinkish brown, and a faint drift of basil across its surface makes it a sight to be remembered.

The flavor is pleasantly—but not overpoweringly—tomato, and the hint of basil adds just a little piquancy. It's a lovely bread to serve with salad, and it makes excellent meat or cheese sandwiches.

½ liter	2 cups tomato juice
	2 tablespoons butter or margarine
	1 tablespoon (1 packet) active dry yeast
	2 teaspoons salt
	2 teaspoons dried basil (or 4 teaspoons finely chopped fresh basil)
	2 tablespoons sugar
about 1½ liters	about 6 cups unbleached white flour
	1 egg beaten with 1 tablespoon water
	extra basil for topping

Put the tomato juice and butter into a saucepan and heat on top of the stove until the juice feels comfortably warm when you stick your finger in it. Remove the pan from the heat and stir until the butter is melted.

Pour the mixture into a large bowl and add the yeast, salt, basil, sugar, and 2 cups of flour. Beat with a wooden spoon until the mixture is perfectly smooth. Continue to add flour until the dough is stiff enough to knead.

Knead for about 5 minutes, until the dough is smooth and springy. Put it into an oiled bowl and turn it over so that the oiled side is up. Cover it and put it in a warm place to rise until it has doubled in bulk.

Punch down the dough and knead it for a minute or two to break any large bubbles. Cut it in half with a knife. Form each piece of dough into a loaf shape and put it into a buttered medium-size loaf pan—8 × 4 inches. Cover the pans and put them in a warm place. When the loaves have doubled in bulk, paint them with the egg glaze and sprinkle them with basil. Bake in a preheated oven at 375°F for about 30 minutes, or until the breads are very brown and sound hollow when tapped on the bottom. Remove from pans and cool on racks.

This is similar to French and other Mediterranean breads, but it is especially easy to make and can be done in very little time. Traditionally, it is made with all white flour, but the addition of some whole-wheat flour gives more flavor and character. You can replace the whole-wheat flour with white if you prefer.

CUBAN BREAD

	2 tablespoons (2 packets) active dry yeast
½ liter	2 cups whole-wheat flour
¾–1 liter	3–4 cups unbleached white flour
	1 tablespoon salt
	2 tablespoons sugar
½ liter	2 cups warm water (43–46°C, 110–115°F)
	corn meal

Put the yeast, whole-wheat flour, 2 cups of white flour, the salt, and the sugar into a large bowl. Add the warm water and stir well with a wooden spoon.

Add 1 cup more of flour and begin to knead. Add more flour as necessary to make the dough stiff enough to handle easily. Knead for 5 or 6 minutes, until the dough is smooth and elastic.

Grease the bowl, put in the dough, and turn it over so that the greased side is up. Cover it and put it in a warm place to rise until it has doubled in bulk—about 15 minutes.

Punch down the dough and cut it in half with a sharp knife. Slam each piece hard on the table or counter and squeeze it to force out the bubbles. Flatten the dough slightly, then roll it up tightly to form either rounds or submarine-shaped loaves. Slash each one down the middle with a sharp knife.

Sprinkle a baking sheet with corn meal and put the loaves on it. Brush the tops with cold water and put the pan into a cold oven. Turn the oven on at 400°F. The bread will rise as the oven heats up.

Bake for about 50 minutes or until the bread is brown and crispy. For a more authentic crust, put a pan of hot water in the bottom of the oven during baking.

As soon as the bread is finished, remove it from the pan and put it on wire racks to cool.

ROADSIDE POTATO BREAD

What roadsides have to do with a delicious white bread is a mystery, but since the bread always seems to be labeled with this quaint name, we may as well go along with the custom. Perhaps the person who first thought it up did so while walking along the side of a road—or maybe he or she sold the bread at a roadside stand.

In any case, the bread really does contain potatoes; you can just ignore the roadside part. In older recipes, the potatoes were always freshly boiled and mashed, and the cooking liquid was added to the dough. You can still follow that method if you choose, but for those who prefer the convenience, instant mashed potatoes substitute for the real thing, and milk (made from powder) takes the place of potato water.

Potato bread is a particularly fine and tender bread; it has an excellent crust and a very moist, dense, light crumb. The recipe makes three medium loaves or two very large ones. This is a good bread to make in big round casseroles or in coffee cans; if you use either, be sure to dust some corn meal in the bottoms and on the sides after you grease them, and don't fill the containers much more than halfway. If you use conventional loaf pans, you can just use oil or butter on them and skip the corn meal.

¼ liter

1 cup mashed potatoes
2 tablespoons (2 packets) active dry
    yeast
3 tablespoons honey

¾ liter	3 cups warm water (43–46°C, 110–115° F)
¼ liter	1 cup nonfat dry milk powder
	3 tablespoons oil
	4 teaspoons salt
2–2½ liters	8–10 cups unbleached white flour

(NOTE: If you use instant potato powder or flakes, consult the package directions to find out how much you have to use to make the required amount; then mix the potatoes *only* with water; skip the milk but after you measure the amount of water called for, add additional water equal to the specified amount of milk; the liquid will add up to close to 1 cup. You need not make it hot (if you did, you would have to wait for it to cool), but only lukewarm. Omit the butter and seasoning. In brief, you want to mix enough dried potato with enough warm water to make 1 cup of mashed potatoes.)

In a large bowl, mix together the potatoes, yeast, honey, water, milk powder, oil, salt, and 6 cups of flour. Beat well with a wooden spoon, then add 2 more cups of flour. Use more if necessary to make a good, kneadable dough.

Knead the dough until it is perfectly smooth and very elastic. Grease the bowl, put in the dough and turn it over. Cover with plastic wrap or a towel and put it in a warm place to rise until the dough has doubled in bulk.

Punch down the dough and allow it to rise a second time. Punch it down again, cut it into the number of portions you need, and shape it into loaves. Put them into their pans, cover them, and let them rise until double in bulk again.

Meanwhile, preheat the oven to 375°F. Bake the bread for 30 to 45 minutes (depending on the size of the loaves), or until it is very brown and sounds hollow when tapped on the bottom. Remove from pans and cool on racks.

CARAWAY POTATO BREAD

Here is another potato bread. This one uses no oil and less milk, so the texture is somewhat different. It is interestingly flavored with caraway seeds. The recipe makes a particularly impressive loaf when it is baked in a large, round container. Use a 12-inch casserole, cake pan, or skillet (if it has a bakeproof handle). For two smaller rounds, use containers that are 8 inches in diameter.

¼ liter	1 cup mashed potatoes
¾ liter	3 cups warm water (43–46°C, 110–115°F)
	1 tablespoon honey
	2 tablespoons (2 packets) active dry yeast
120 milliliters	½ cup nonfat dry milk powder
	1½ tablespoons salt
	1½ tablespoons caraway seeds
2–2½ liters	8–10 cups unbleached white flour

(NOTE: For preparing mashed potatoes from instant potatoes, *see* directions in Roadside Potato Bread recipe, page 47.)

Put the first seven ingredients into a large bowl and add 4 cups of flour. Beat well with a wooden spoon.

Add 4 more cups of flour and begin to knead. Add more flour as necessary to keep the dough from sticking.

Knead for about 8 minutes or until the dough is smooth and elastic. Put it into a greased bowl and turn it greased side up. Cover it and put in a warm place to rise until it has doubled in bulk.

Punch down the dough, cut it in half and make two round balls —or make one large ball for a single loaf. Put the loaves into their greased pans or casseroles, cover them, and let them rise until they have doubled in bulk.

Brush the tops of the loaves with cold water and bake them in a preheated 400°F oven for about 45 minutes. Brush once with cold water midway in the baking period for an extra crunchy crust.

When the bread is dark brown and makes a hollow sound when you rap it on the bottom, remove it from the pans and cool it on a wire rack.

BASIC SWEET DOUGH

This sweet yeast dough is basic in the same sense that Basic White Bread is basic: with minor variations, it is the basis for a great variety of buns and coffee cakes.

If you like, you can double (or even triple) the recipe, use a portion, and store the rest in a plastic bag in the refrigerator. It will keep well for three or four days. It will probably rise a little, so be sure to punch it down before you use it.

	1 tablespoon (1 packet) active dry yeast
120 milliliters	**½ cup warm water (43–46°C, 110–115°F)**
80 milliliters	**⅓ cup nonfat dry milk powder**
	4 tablespoons sugar
	½ teaspoon salt
	1 egg
½ liter, plus up to 120 milliliters more	**2–2½ cups unbleached white flour**
	4 tablespoons very soft butter

If you are making a single recipe, you can use an ordinary large mixing bowl; if you are going to double or triple the recipe, use the dishpan method—or knead on a board.

Mix all the ingredients together, using just enough flour to make a dough that you can knead. Knead it for about 5 minutes.

Put the ball of dough into an oiled bowl and turn the dough oiled side up. Cover it and let it rise in a warm place until it has doubled in bulk. Punch down the dough and use it in any of the following variations. (If you are going to store any of the dough, now is the time to do it.)

❋ ❋

Press the dough into a greased 8 × 8-inch pan. Mix together with your fingertips: **CRUMB CAKE**

120 milliliters	**½ cup white flour**
80 milliliters	**⅓ cup sugar**
	1 teaspoon cinnamon
	4 tablespoons (½ stick) butter or margarine

When the mixture is well blended and crumbly, sprinkle it evenly over the top of the dough. Cover the pan and let the dough rise until it has doubled in bulk. Bake the cake in a preheated oven at 375°F for about 20 minutes or until well browned.

𝕮𝕮

CARAMEL ROLLS (SCHNECKEN)

Schnecken is the German word for snails.

	8 tablespoons (1 stick) butter or margarine
120 milliliters	**½ cup brown sugar**
120 milliliters	**½ cup broken pecans or sliced almonds**

Filling

	2 tablespoons softened butter or margarine
	1–2 teaspoons cinnamon
120 milliliters	**½ cup raisins (optional)**

Melt the 8 tablespoons of butter or margarine in a round pan (you can use a skillet if it has a heatproof or detachable handle) about 10 inches in diameter. Mix the brown sugar with the melted butter and spread it evenly over the bottom of the pan. Sprinkle the nuts over the mixture.

Roll the dough on a very lightly floured board into a rectangle about 8 × 16 inches. Spread it with the softened butter or margarine. Sprinkle the cinnamon (and raisins, if used) over the top.

Caramel Rolls

Starting at one of the long sides, carefully roll up the dough like a jelly roll, keeping it as even as possible. Pinch the seam together tightly.

Slice the roll into 1-inch slices and place them, cut side down, on top of the mixture in the round pan. Cover, and let the buns rise to double their size. They will all be touching each other now. Bake them at 350°F for about 30 minutes or until they are well browned.

As soon as you remove the pan from the oven, put a large plate on top of it and invert it to turn out the rolls.

⚘⚘

	2 tablespoons soft butter or margarine	SWEDISH TEA RING
120 milliliters	½ cup brown sugar	
	2 teaspoons cinnamon	
120 milliliters	½ cup raisins or currants—or a mixture of both	

On a lightly floured board, roll the dough into a rectangle about 8 × 16 inches. Spread it with soft butter and sprinkle the other ingredients evenly over the top.

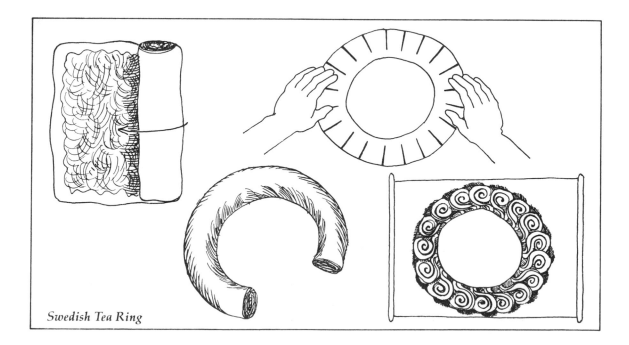

Swedish Tea Ring

Starting at one of the long sides, roll up the dough tightly and pinch the seam together. If necessary, shape and pull the roll until it has about the same diameter all over. Carefully lift it onto a greased baking sheet and join the two ends to form a ring. Pinch it closed.

Now take a pair of kitchen shears—or any large, clean scissors —and make cuts along the outer edge of the ring. Cut a little more than halfway into the center and make a cut about every inch. When you have finished making the cuts, lift each "petal" and turn it on its side.

Cover the ring and put it in a warm place to rise. When it has doubled in bulk, heat the oven to 375°F. Bake the ring for 20 to 25 minutes, until it is quite brown. When it is cool, ice it with Confectioner's Sugar Icing:

CONFECTIONER'S SUGAR ICING

¼ liter

1 cup confectioner's sugar
about 1 tablespoon milk
a few drops of vanilla or other
    flavoring (almond, lemon, or
    orange)

Mix all the ingredients together in a small bowl until the icing is perfectly smooth. If it is too thick to spread, add more milk, one drop at a time, until the icing is just right. If it is too thin, add more sugar, one tablespoon at a time.

While the icing is still soft, you can decorate the ring with nuts, candied cherries or other fruit, or dots of jelly.

紫紫

JAM BUNS

fruit jam
1 egg white
confectioner's sugar

Let the dough rise until it is very light. Roll it about ½ inch thick and cut it into circles or squares, each about 3 inches across. To make circles, use a floured biscuit cutter, the rim of a glass or a can.

Put the buns on a well-greased baking sheet and with your thumb make a deep well in the center of each one. Fill the well with jam.

Beat 1 egg white until it is stiff and paint the top of each bun with it, using a pastry brush. Sprinkle with confectioner's sugar and bake at 375°F for about 20 minutes.

Jam Buns

✼✼

120 milliliters	½ **cup currants**	**HOT CROSS BUNS**
	melted butter	
120 milliliters	½ **cup milk**	
	1 tablespoon sugar	
	Confectioner's Sugar Icing	

When you are ready to knead the dough in the basic recipe, add ½ cup of currants.

After the dough has risen, punch it down and shape it into balls the size of Ping-Pong balls. Put them fairly close together (but not touching) in a buttered cake pan. Brush the tops with melted butter and let the balls begin to rise. When they have risen a bit, cut a cross into the top of each one with a single-edge razor blade or a sharp knife.

Let the buns continue to rise until they are two and a half times their original size. Bake them at 375°F for about 20 minutes.

Hot Cross Buns

Take them out of the oven and brush them with ½ cup of milk that has been sweetened with 1 tablespoon of sugar, then put them back into the oven for another 2 minutes. Remove them, cool, and fill the cross with Confectioner's Sugar Icing (page 52).

※ ※

TURNOVERS   Roll out the dough on a floured board until it is about ¼ inch thick. Cut it into 3-inch squares and put 1 tablespoonful of jam or any of the following fillings in the center of each square. Lift the corners, bring them together over the center of the filling, and pinch them securely together. You can wet the corners with a little cold water to make sure that they stick.

Put the turnovers on a greased baking sheet and let them rise until they have doubled in bulk. Bake at 400°F until they are well browned, for 20 to 30 minutes or more, depending on the kind of filling.

FILLINGS FOR TURNOVERS

Walnut Filling

½ liter   **2 cups ground or chopped walnuts**
60 milliliters   **¼ cup sugar**
60 milliliters   **¼ cup honey**

Mix all the ingredients together to form a paste.

Prune Filling

½ kilogram   **1 pound prunes**
120 milliliters   **½ cup sugar**
                 1 tablespoon lemon juice

Boil the prunes in a little water until they are very soft. Remove the pits (if any) and rub the prunes through a colander or put them into a food processor. Mix the purée with the sugar and lemon juice.

Apricot Filling

Follow the direction for Prune Filling, using apricots instead of prunes.

Turnovers

Almond Filling

120 milliliters	½ cup ground or finely chopped almonds
	3 tablespoons butter, at room temperature
	1 teaspoon grated lemon rind
	1 egg, beaten

Mix all the ingredients together, using just enough of the egg to make a stiff paste.

WHOLE-GRAIN BREADS

Here is a comparison of whole-wheat flour with enriched white flour, from *Composition of Foods* (Agricultural Handbook No. 8, United States Department of Agriculture).

	Whole Wheat (per 100 g)		Enriched White (per 100 g)	
PROTEIN	13.3	g	10.5	g
MINERALS				
Calcium	41	mg	16	mg
Phosphorus	372	mg	87	mg
Iron	3.3	mg	2.9	mg
Potassium	370	mg	95	mg
Sodium	3	mg	2	mg
VITAMINS				
Thiamin	.55	mg	.44	mg
Riboflavin	.12	mg	.26	mg
Niacin	4.3	mg	3.5	mg

This table tells you most of what you need to know intellectually about the value of whole-grain bread as compared to white bread; the *non*intellectual appreciation comes with the eating!

This is a fine, hearty, chewy bread that is full of nutrition and has a good, rich, nutty flavor. It is an all-purpose bread that makes marvelous toast and sandwiches and also keeps very well.

HONEY WHOLE-WHEAT BREAD

2 tablespoons (2 packets) active dry yeast

½ liter plus 120 milliliters

2½ cups warm water (43–46°C, 110–115°F)

4 tablespoons honey

1 tablespoon salt

4 tablespoons oil

2–2½ liters

8–10 cups whole-wheat flour

Put the yeast into a large bowl and stir in the water, honey, salt, oil, and 6 cups of flour. Beat well with a wooden spoon until thoroughly blended, then add 2 more cups of flour. Mix the dough with your hands, then begin to squeeze it down with your fist. Add more flour until the dough is stiff enough to knead.

Whole-wheat flour contains less gluten than white flour so it is not quite as easy to work with. Keep kneading, pressing with the heel of your hand, folding the dough over and turning it once in a while. It will not get quite as smooth and shiny as white flour dough, but it will become bouncy and resistant and will come away from your hand and the bowl easily; it should take about 10 minutes or so to reach that stage.

Oil the bowl; put in the dough and turn it over oily side up, then cover it and put it in a warm place to rise. When it has doubled in bulk (about 1 hour), knead it for another minute or two before you shape it for the pans. The recipe will make two very large loaves or three smaller ones. It also works nicely in casseroles or coffee cans. Grease the containers and if you use cans or casseroles sprinkle a little corn meal on the bottom just to make sure you have no removal problems. Make loaves that fill the containers halfway.

When the loaves have doubled in bulk, heat the oven to 375°F and bake them for about 40 minutes. The bread should be *very* brown (darker than white bread) and sound hollow when tapped on the bottom. Remove the bread from the pans at once and cool it on wire racks.

₩ *VARIATIONS* ₩

NOTE: Try adding 1 egg to the dough when you add the water. It makes a "cakier" texture.

LIGHT WHOLE-WHEAT BREAD

For a lighter whole-wheat bread, use half whole-wheat flour, half unbleached white. It doesn't have to be exactly half and half; use white for 4 cups, whole-wheat for all the rest.

BRAN BREAD

Add 1 cup of bran after you beat the dough with a spoon.

RAISIN BRAN BREAD

Add bran, as above, plus 1 cup of raisins.

75-MINUTE HEALTH BREAD

This recipe is based (loosely) on one developed by a Danish scientist during World War II. It is very rich in protein and low in fat, and can be served—start to finish—in an hour and a quarter. *Can* be doesn't necessarily mean it *will* be; if you are a totally inexperienced baker, you might do better to plan on an hour and a half (still pretty fast for a kneaded yeast bread!).

This is a remarkably good, chewy bread, one you might well make your daily bread.

The recipe makes three small loaves or two large ones.

	3 tablespoons (3 packets) active dry yeast
120 milliliters	½ cup warm water (43–46°C, 110–115°F)
¼ liter plus 80 milliliters	1⅓ cups (one 1-quart packet) nonfat dry milk powder
½ liter	2 cups warm water (43–46°C, 110–115°F)

	1 tablespoon honey
	1 tablespoon salt
¼ liter	1 cup wheat germ
½ liter	2 cups whole-wheat flour
¾–1 liter	3–4 cups unbleached white flour

To get the yeast started as quickly as possible, warm the bowl by rinsing it with hot water and drying it; immediately put in the yeast, ½ cup warm water, and a drop or two of the honey.

Assemble the other ingredients, then add the milk powder, water, honey, salt, wheat germ, and whole-wheat flour. Beat 100 strokes with a wooden spoon.

Add 3 cups of white flour and mix. Add as much more as necessary in order to knead the dough. If it is very sticky at first, knead with your fist until it begins to shape up, taking care to scrape the bottom and sides of the bowl often. Knead for about 10 minutes. The dough will still be looser than usual.

Oil the loaf pans (three small ones will make the baking time a little shorter than two standard pans) and divide the dough into them. If it is too sticky to shape nicely, wet your hand with cold water and smooth the tops into a loaf shape. Make a slit down the center of each loaf with a sharp knife.

Put the pans into a cold oven and set the temperature for 150°F; set the timer for 15 minutes. By the end of that time, the dough should have doubled in size. If it hasn't, wait until it does. Then change the heat setting to 350°F and continue baking until the loaves are well browned and sound hollow when tapped on the bottom—about 45 minutes. Turn out on racks to cool.

PEASANT BREAD

It would be hard to say just what kind of peasant made this bread first, but it is typical of many of the country breads of Europe, especially in the middle and eastern sectors.

This is a bread to have when you're really hungry; a couple of slices with a good bowl of soup are all you need for a complete meal. The loaf has a hard, crunchy crust and a coarse, hearty, dark-colored crumb.

	2 tablespoons (2 packets) active dry yeast
½ liter	2 cups warm water (43–46°C, 110–115°F)
½ liter plus 120 milliliters	2½ cups lukewarm coffee, either leftover or freshly made instant
120 milliliters	½ cup yellow corn meal
	1½ tablespoons salt
2½ liters plus	10 cups (or more) whole-wheat flour

Put the yeast, water, coffee, corn meal, salt, and most of the flour into a large bowl. Stir with a wooden spoon until the mixture leaves the sides of the bowl; let it rest for 10 minutes.

Use the rest of the flour to sprinkle over the dough and on your hands as you begin to knead. Knead for 10 minutes, adding more flour if the dough is too sticky to turn or fold. Oil the bowl, put in the dough, turn it over, and cover it with a clean dish towel that has been wrung out in cold water. Put the dough in a warm place to rise. When it has doubled in bulk, punch it down and let it rise a second time.

When the dough has doubled in bulk again, knead it for a minute or two. Form it into a ball and cut it in half with a knife. Make two round loaves and put them on an ungreased baking sheet that has been sprinkled with corn meal.

Brush the tops of the loaves with cold water and let them rise for 20 minutes. Then brush the tops with cold water again; slash a cross on them with a sharp knife, and bake them at 375°F for about 1 hour.

When the bread is dark brown and hollow-sounding, put it on wire racks to cool.

Note: Instead of two large rounds, the recipe will make two very long loaves (as long as the baking sheet), or four small ones. Make four diagonal slashes on long loaves.

This is another hearty, wholesome bread with a delicious, nut-like flavor. You can buy wheat berries in any health-food store or in any market that sells whole grains. Few people will be able to identify them in the bread.

WHEAT-BERRY BREAD

120 milliliters	½ cup wheat berries
¼ liter	1 cup boiling water
¼ liter	1 cup cold water
½ liter	2 cups warm water (43–46°C, 110–115°F)
	3 tablespoons (3 packets) active dry yeast
120 milliliters	½ cup honey
	1 tablespoon salt
60 milliliters	¼ cup oil
2 liters	8 cups whole-wheat flour
½–1 liter	2–4 cups unbleached white flour

Put the wheat berries with the boiling water in a saucepan and simmer until all the water is absorbed—about 20 minutes. Add the cold water and transfer the mixture to a large bowl. Add the warm water, yeast, and all the other ingredients except the white flour.

Mix the dough thoroughly with a wooden spoon, then add half the white flour and begin to knead. Keep adding flour until the dough is easy to handle and will keep its shape. Knead for 7 to 8 minutes.

Put the dough into a greased bowl and turn it greased side up. Cover it and put it in a warm place to rise until it has doubled in bulk—about 1 hour.

Punch down the dough, knead it briefly to break any large bubbles, and cut it in half. Make two round loaves and put them on a baking sheet that has been sprinkled with corn meal. Use a sharp knife to cut a cross in the center of each loaf.

Put the pan into a cold oven and turn on the heat to 350°F. Bake for about 1 hour or until the bread is brown and sounds hollow when tapped on the bottom.

For an extra-crisp crust, brush the loaves with cold water several times during baking.

Cool on racks.

CORN-WHEAT BREAD

This is an unusually heavy, dense, moist loaf that is similar to Peasant Bread—but different. It keeps well and is good at any time. It makes a particularly satisfying breakfast bread that's guaranteed to stick to your ribs all morning.

¼ liter	1 cup boiling water
120 milliliters	½ cup yellow corn meal
¼ liter plus 120 milliliters	1½ cups cold water
	1 tablespoon salt
	2 tablespoons (2 packets) active dry yeast
	3 tablespoons brown sugar
80 milliliters	⅓ cup nonfat dry milk powder
1¼–1½ liters	5–6 cups whole-wheat flour

Add the corn meal to the boiling water in a saucepan. Reduce the heat and simmer, stirring constantly, for 2 to 3 minutes, or until mixture is very thick.

Put the mixture into a large bowl and add the cold water. Stir, then add the salt, yeast, sugar, milk powder, and 3 cups of whole-wheat flour. Beat with a wooden spoon or an electric mixer until there are no corn-meal lumps.

Add 2 cups of flour—or more if necessary in order to knead. This tends to be a sticky dough that is never really easy to handle, but don't be put off by it; it's all that corn-meal mush that makes it mushy.

Knead the dough for 6 or 7 minutes, then put it into a greased bowl; turn, greased side up, cover it, and leave it in a warm place to rise until it has doubled in bulk.

After the dough has risen, it is much more manageable, so punch it down and knead it for a few minutes more. Cut it in half, shape it into two loaves and put them into greased 9- × -5-inch loaf pans. Cover and let rise until doubled in bulk—nearly to the tops of the pans.

Preheat the oven to 375°F and bake for 45 minutes or until the bread is very brown and sounds hollow when rapped on the bottom.

Remove it from the pans and cool it on wire racks.

This is a dark oatmeal bread, chewy and slightly sweet. It goes well with jam for breakfast or teatime and makes excellent toast. It keeps well, too. If you prefer less sweetening, just cut the amount of molasses in half.

OATMEAL BREAD

¼ liter plus 120 milliliters	1½ cups oats (not instant)
½ liter	2 cups boiling water
	1 tablespoon (1 packet) active dry yeast
120 milliliters	½ cup warm water (43–46°C, 110–115°F)
60 milliliters	¼ cup molasses
60 milliliters	¼ cup oil
	1 tablespoon salt
½ liter	2 cups unbleached white flour
½–¾ liter	2–3 cups whole-wheat flour

Put the oats into a large bowl and pour the boiling water over them. Stir and set aside.

Mix the yeast with the warm water. When the oats mixture has cooled to lukewarm, add the yeast, molasses, oil, salt, and white flour. Beat well with a wooden spoon.

Add 2 cups of whole-wheat flour and begin to knead. Add more flour as necessary until the dough is easy to handle. Knead for about 5 minutes.

Cover the bowl and put in a warm place until the dough has doubled in bulk. Punch it down; divide it in half, and shape it into two loaves. Bake them in well-greased medium loaf pans at 350°F. This is a good bread to do in coffee cans, too—1-pound size; if you use cans, don't forget to put corn meal in the bottom after you grease them.

The baking time varies from 45 to 60 minutes, depending on the containers, but the bread is done when the tops are well browned and the loaves sound hollow when tapped.

VARIATIONS

LIGHT OATMEAL BREAD

Use all unbleached white flour instead of part whole-wheat and substitute honey for molasses.

OATMEAL FRUIT BREAD

After the first rising, work into the dough ½ cup chopped walnuts or pecans, and 1 cup cut-up prunes, dates, or dried apricots.

ANADAMA BREAD

There are many different versions of this corn-meal bread—and it's not hard to understand why. An old, old legend traces its beginnings to a New England fisherman and his wife Anna, who had no imagination whatsoever about breakfast. Year in and year out she gave her husband exactly the same breakfast every morning: corn-meal mush. Back in those days it didn't readily occur to a man to cook his *own* breakfast, so our fisherman did nothing but grumble and complain. One day he lost his temper completely, and just before Anna tossed the corn meal into the pot of boiling water that would transform it into the loathsome mush, he snatched it from her hand and dumped it into a bowl. Then, furiously grabbing whatever he could reach in the kitchen, he threw in some molasses, flour, and so forth, and proceeded to make himself what turned out to be a delicious bread. All the time he was kneading the dough he kept muttering, "Anna, damn her!"

	1 tablespoon (1 packet) active dry yeast
¼ liter plus 120 milliliters	1½ cups warm water (43–46°C, 110–115°F)
	2 tablespoons oil
60 milliliters	¼ cup molasses
	1 tablespoon salt
120 milliliters	½ cup yellow corn meal
½ liter	2 cups unbleached white flour
½ liter plus	2 cups or more whole-wheat flour

Stir the yeast with the water in a large bowl. Add the oil, molasses, salt, corn meal, and white flour. Beat well with a wooden spoon.

Add 2 cups of whole-wheat flour and work it into the dough. Add a little more flour if necessary in order to knead.

Knead for about 5 minutes, or until the dough is springy and resistant. It will not become very smooth because of the grainy corn meal.

Put the dough into an oiled bowl and turn it over. Cover it and put it in a warm place to rise until it has doubled in bulk, about 1 hour.

Punch down the dough, cut it in two, and shape it into loaves. Bake in well-greased pans—about 8 × 4 inches—at 425°F for 10 minutes, then turn down the heat to 350°F and bake for about 35 minutes more. The bread should be brown and sound hollow when tapped. Turn out onto racks immediately.

SPROUTED WHEAT BREAD

The sprouts in this bread give it a most unusual flavor and a fascinating texture: it looks as if it needed a shave. It is also rich in vitamins and is very, very good for you. Although you can buy ready-made wheat sprouts in some places, it's fun to make your own. Here's how to do it.

⚜ ⚜

THE SPROUTS

Put about 4 tablespoons of wheat berries (or kernels) into a colander or large strainer and rinse them under cold running water. Set the colander or strainer into a large bowl (to catch the drips) and cover the whole thing with a kitchen towel. Put it out of the way in a warm corner of the kitchen and leave it for about three days.

Each day you will have to water the sprouts three or four times; after meals and at bedtime is an easy routine to remember. Just hold the container under running water for a few seconds to rinse the sprouts, then put it back in the bowl and keep the berries warm and dark under the towel. By the end of the third day they should be well sprouted and ready for use.

Taste them and you will be surprised at their sweetness; as the berries sprout, much of their wheat starch is converted to sugar. If you have more sprouts than you need for the bread, keep them in a plastic bag in the refrigerator. They are good for snacks, or as an ingredient in salads, omelets, or other food. They will keep for several days.

You can use the same method for making other kinds of sprouts. Sprouted mung beans are the familiar sprouts of Chinese dishes, and they are good in all kinds of egg, meat, and seafood dishes as well as in bread. You can also sprout sesame and sunflower seeds, lentils, soybeans, alfalfa, and chickpeas.

👐👐

THE BREAD

	2 tablespoons (2 packets) active dry yeast
¾ liter	3 cups warm water (43–46°C, 110–115°F)
	1 tablespoon salt
	3 tablespoons honey
¾ liter plus 120 milliliters	3½ cups unbleached white flour
½ liter	2 cups wheat sprouts
1–1¼ liters	4–5 cups whole-wheat flour

Put everything except the whole-wheat flour into a large mixing bowl and beat with a wooden spoon until the mixture is well blended. Add 2 cups of whole-wheat flour and beat some more. Continue to add whole-wheat flour until the dough is just stiff enough to handle. It should remain slightly sticky.

Knead for about 10 minutes, then put the dough into a greased bowl and turn it greased side up. Cover it and put it in a warm place to rise until it has doubled in bulk.

Punch the dough down, knead it for a minute or two, then divide it into two or three parts; it will make two large bread loaves, or will fill three 1-pound coffee cans (when it has risen, of course).

Butter the cans or pans (corn-meal the bottoms of cans in addition) and put in the dough. Let it rise until it has doubled in bulk. Bake it for about 1 hour at 350°F. When the bread is done it will be very brown and sound hollow when rapped on the bottom. Turn it out to cool on wire racks.

WHEATENA WHEAT BREAD

Try a couple of slices of this bread for breakfast instead of a bowl of cereal. It's every bit as nutritious and may make a pleasant change.

This is not strictly a breakfast bread, of course, but one that you can enjoy at any time. The added cereal provides a nutty crunchiness that is virtually irresistible.

160 milliliters	**⅔ cup nonfat dry milk powder**
¾ liter	**3 cups warm water (43–46°C, 110–115°F)**
	2 tablespoons (2 packets) active dry yeast
¼ liter	**1 cup raw Wheatena**
	2 tablespoons honey
	1 tablespoon salt
	2 tablespoons oil
1½–2 liters	**6–8 cups whole-wheat flour**

In a large bowl, mix the first seven ingredients and 3 cups of whole-wheat flour. Beat well with a wooden spoon. Add 3 cups more of flour and begin to knead. Add as much more flour as you need to make a dough that is easy to handle.

Knead for 8 to 10 minutes, or until the dough is very elastic. Put it into a greased bowl and turn it over. Cover the dough and put it in a warm place to rise until it has doubled in bulk.

Punch down the dough, knead it for a minute, then cut it in two. Shape each half into a loaf and put it into a greased large pan— 9 × 5 inches. Slit each loaf down the middle with a sharp knife. Cover the pans and let the dough rise until it has doubled in bulk. Brush the loaves with cold water and bake them at 400°F for about 40 minutes, or until they are brown and hollow-sounding when tapped. Turn them out to cool on racks.

SOY BREAD

Soy flour is milled from soybeans, one of our richest vegetable sources of protein. Since even a small amount of soy flour adds greatly to the nutritional value of any bread, this one almost qualifies as a meal in itself. It also happens to have a distinctive and magnificent flavor.

Because soy flour is lacking in gluten, it makes a sticky dough which is worked in a rather unconventional manner.

	2 tablespoons (2 packets) active dry yeast
160 milliliters	⅔ cup nonfat dry milk powder
½ liter plus 120 milliliters	2½ cups warm water (43–46°C, 110–115°F)
60 milliliters	¼ cup oil
80 milliliters	⅓ cup honey
	1½ tablespoons salt
¼ liter	1 cup unbleached white flour
¼ liter plus 80 milliliters	1⅓ cups soy flour
1–1¼ liters	4–5 cups whole-wheat flour

Mix all the ingredients, in the order given, in a large bowl, using 4 cups whole-wheat flour; put the rest where it is handy to reach because you are going to have very sticky hands.

Sprinkle a little flour on top of the dough and knead it just long enough to mix it thoroughly; you won't be able to do much more than that.

Oil the bowl and put in the dough; turn it once, cover it and put it in a warm place to rise until it has doubled in bulk. The dough will be a little easier to handle after the rising. Punch it down and add enough flour to make it easy to knead. Knead until the dough becomes smooth and springy. Then cut it in half, flatten each piece into a rectangle and roll it into a loaf shape.

Put the loaves into medium-size pans (8 × 4 inches) which have been well greased and sprinkled with a little corn meal. Cover the loaves and let them rise until they have doubled in bulk. Preheat the oven to 375°F and bake the bread for 35 to 40 minutes, or until it is very brown and sounds hollow when rapped on the bottom. Turn it out on racks to cool.

NORWEGIAN RYE BREAD

Rye flour is always somewhat hard to work because it makes a very sticky dough—but rye-bread fanciers will find the small extra trouble worth while. This particular bread is fine-grained, smooth, and light-colored and is interestingly flavored with cardamom, which gives it a slightly exotic taste. It goes well with anything but particularly lends itself to cream cheese and/or jam.

	2 tablespoons (2 packets) active dry yeast
½ liter plus 60 milliliters	**2½ cups warm water (43–46°C, 110–115°F)**
	2 tablespoons sugar
160 milliliters	**⅔ cup nonfat dry milk powder**
	4 tablespoons oil
¼ liter	**1 cup wheat germ**
¾ liter plus 120 milliliters	**3½ cups unbleached white flour**
	½ teaspoon powdered cardamom
	1 tablespoon salt
½–¾ liter	**2–3 cups rye flour**
	1 egg white mixed with 1 tablespoon cold water

Use a large bowl and put in all the ingredients except the rye flour and the egg-white mixture. Beat with an electric mixer (or by hand with a wooden spoon) for 3 minutes.

Add 2 cups of rye flour and mix it in with your hand. If it is too sticky to knead, add more flour until you can handle the dough. Knead for about 5 minutes, or longer if necessary, until the dough is smooth and elastic. Cover the bowl and put it in a warm place.

When the dough has risen to double its bulk, punch it down and cut it in half. Form each half into a round loaf by slapping it down hard on the table or counter top; keep slapping and turning, shaping the sides with the palms of your hands all the while. Make the round higher in the center than at the sides. Leave the tops textured for a rugged look, or smooth them with a little cold water.

Put the loaves into round cake or pie pans 8 inches in diameter. Slash a cross into the top of each loaf and let it rise until it has doubled in bulk. (You can make five or six slashes radiating like petals from the center, instead.) Paint the loaves with egg-white glaze. Preheat the oven to 400°F and bake the bread for 30 to 35 minutes, or until it is brown and hollow-sounding when tapped. Turn it out to cool on racks.

POTATO-RYE BREAD

A light, tender rye with the particularly fine texture of potato bread. The potatoes add moistness, too, and so this bread keeps especially well.

To prepare the mashed potatoes from instant powder or flakes, follow the package directions for making one cup, but instead of using boiling water and milk, use warm water for *all* the liquid called for; omit the butter and salt.

¼ liter	1 cup mashed potatoes (fresh or instant)
½ liter plus 60 milliliters	1¼ cups warm water (43–46°C, 110–115°F)
	1 tablespoon salt
	4 tablespoons molasses
	1 tablespoon caraway seeds
	1 tablespoon (1 packet) active dry yeast
¼ liter plus 120 milliliters	1½ cups rye flour
½–¾ liter	2–3 cups unbleached white flour
	1 egg white mixed with 1 tablespoon cold water

Put everything up to and including the rye flour into a large bowl and beat well with a wooden spoon. Add 2 cups white flour and as much more as is necessary to make a soft dough that you can knead. It will be sticky, so keep sprinkling flour on your hands and on the dough each time you turn it and fold it over.

Knead for 5 to 7 minutes, until the dough becomes springy, then put it into a greased bowl and turn it greased side up. Cover the dough and let it rise in a warm place until it has doubled in bulk.

Punch down the dough and knead it for 2 to 3 minutes. Butter a casserole or round, deep cake pan and sprinkle a little corn meal on the bottom; tilt the vessel so that the meal sticks to the sides as well.

Shape the dough into a round and put it into the pan. Cover it and let it rise until it has doubled in bulk.

When the loaf is ready for the oven, brush it with the egg-white glaze and bake it at 375°F for about 40 minutes. The bread should be dark brown and sound hollow when tapped on the bottom. Remove it from the pan at once and put it on a wire rack to cool.

A dense, hearty bread, surely one of the best in the world. Use about three fairly large potatoes to make one cup of mashed—and be sure to let them cool to lukewarm before you use them. To prepare the mashed potatoes from instant powder or flakes, follow the package directions for making one cup, but instead of boiling water and milk, use warm water for *all* the liquid called for; omit the butter and salt.

RYE-CORN-POTATO BREAD

¼ liter	1 cup yellow corn meal
¼ liter plus 120 milliliters	1½ cups cold water
¼ liter plus 120 milliliters	1½ cups boiling water
	1 tablespoon (1 packet) active dry yeast
60 milliliters	¼ cup warm water (43–46°C, 110–115°F)
½ liter	2 cups mashed potatoes
	1½ tablespoons salt
	2 tablespoons oil
	1 tablespoon caraway seeds
	1 tablespoon sugar
½ liter	2 cups unbleached white flour
about 1¼ liters	about 5 cups rye flour
	1 egg white mixed with 1 tablespoon cold water

Mix the corn meal and cold water in a saucepan, then add the boiling water and boil for 2 minutes, stirring constantly. Set the mixture aside to cool.

When you are ready to proceed, get out your largest container. If you do not have a dishpan that you regularly use for bread dough, use a large roasting pan. Put in the yeast and warm water; add the potatoes, corn-meal mixture (*not* hot!), salt, oil, caraway seeds, sugar, and white flour. Stir with a wooden spoon and add about half the rye flour. Continue to mix with the spoon, adding more rye flour a little at a time. When you can't mix any more, begin to knead.

The dough will be very heavy, sticky, and hard to handle—but don't give up; just keep kneading until it gets easier. This dough will never be as smooth and elastic as most doughs, but work on it for at least 10 minutes.

Form the dough into a ball, put it into an oiled bowl and turn it greased side up. Cover it and put it in a warm place to rise until it has doubled in bulk.

Punch down the dough and divide it by cutting it with a sharp knife. You can make two giant loaves, or three or four smaller ones. Since they do not have to be contained in pans, you can make them any size or shape you like. Slap each piece of dough hard on the table top a few times and form it into a round, oval, or long shape. Put the loaves on a ungreased baking sheet (or in cake tins) sprinkled with corn meal. If you use a baking sheet, leave plenty of room between the loaves. Cover them and let them rise until not quite doubled in bulk.

Paint the tops with the egg-white glaze and preheat the oven to 350°F. Bake the bread for 1 hour or longer, repeating the egg glaze after ½ hour. When the breads are dark brown and sound hollow when tapped on the bottom, turn them out on wire racks to cool.

PUMPERNICKEL BREAD

It is said that this bread takes its name from the fifteenth-century German baker, Nicholas Pumper. We can't vouch for Herr Pumper, but we are certain that this bread is one of the great German specialties. It is particularly good served with cold cuts or cheese—with plenty of mustard, of course.

This is an uncommonly hard dough to knead, so do it on a day when you are feeling strong and energetic.

	3 tablespoons (3 packets) active dry yeast
¼ liter plus 120 milliliters	1½ cups warm water (43–46°C, 110–115°F)
	4 tablespoons dark molasses
	1⅓ tablespoons (4 teaspoons) salt
	1½ tablespoons caraway seeds

	2 tablespoons oil
½ liter plus 180 milliliters	**2¾ cups rye flour**
	4 tablespoons unsweetened cocoa
½–¾ liter	**2–3 cups unbleached white flour**

Mix the yeast and water in a large bowl. Stir in the molasses, salt, seeds, oil, rye flour, and cocoa. Beat with an electric mixer or a wooden spoon for 2 minutes.

Add 2 cups white flour and mix it in by hand. Add more flour, a little at a time, until the dough is just stiff enough to knead. When you think it is kneadable, stop; cover the dough and let it rest for 10 minutes. (The 10 minutes is not wasted time; use it to put away all your supplies and to put the utensils you used into the sink to soak.)

When the time is up, knead the dough for about 10 minutes. This is as hard work as you will ever come up against in your bread-baking career. Whatever your usual kneading technique, you will probably need two hands to battle this tough, strong lump. When the dough is smooth (and you are exhausted), put it into an oiled bowl and turn it oily side up. Cover it and put it in a warm place to rise until it has doubled in bulk. This will probably take at least an hour, perhaps longer. When the dough is ready, punch it down; cover it, and let it rise again.

After the second rising (which takes about 40 minutes), punch down the dough and cut it in half. Shape each piece into a round loaf or a long one (like a submarine), depending on your whim. Put the loaves on a baking sheet sprinkled with corn meal and let them rise for 1 hour.

Heat the oven to 375°F and bake the bread for 30 to 35 minutes, until it is dark, dark brown and sounds hollow when tapped on the bottom. Cool it on wire racks. While it is still warm, polish the tops with a small lump of butter held in a piece of paper towel.

❧ VARIATIONS ❧

LIGHT PUMPERNICKEL BREAD

Leave out the cocoa, use honey instead of molasses, reduce the rye flour to 2 cups, and use an additional ¾ cup of unbleached white flour.

PUMPERNICKEL ROLLS

After the second rising, divide the dough into twelve or more equal parts and shape them into balls or miniature loaves. Put them on a greased baking sheet and let them rise for 40 minutes. The baking time is the same as for the bread. For variety, you can make one loaf of bread and a batch of rolls at the same time.

BATTER BREADS

NO-KNEAD WHOLE-WHEAT BREAD

When you're in a hurry (or suffering from tennis elbow) but still want a good yeast bread, this is the one to make. It requires no kneading at all and rises very quickly, so the total preparation time is only about half that of Honey Whole-Wheat Bread.

This one has honey in it too, and it tastes just as good as the other, although it has a coarser texture. Its only disadvantage is that it doesn't keep as well, so unless you plan to use both loaves promptly, wrap one as soon as it's cold, and freeze it.

Because this dough is very soft and sticky it doesn't leave its pans without a struggle—unless you take special precautions; if you have Teflon-coated pans, butter them and use them. If you have plain pans or want to use casseroles or any other kind of containers, butter them heavily and sprinkle well with corn meal to avoid problems.

This is a good standard bread to whip up in a hurry when you have unexpected guests, or to eat as your daily bread if you don't have much time to spend in the kitchen.

	3 tablespoons (3 packets) active dry yeast
1 liter	4 cups warm water (43–46°C, 110–115°F)
	4 tablespoons honey
	1½ tablespoons salt
1¾ liters plus 120 milliliters	7½ cups whole-wheat flour

Put all the ingredients into a regular mixing bowl and beat

well with a wooden spoon for several minutes; since you are not going to knead this dough, the beating and the rising are the only workouts it will get.

Pour the batter directly into prepared pans (two large loaf pans), cover and let rise until a little less than double in bulk; if you use standard pans, the dough will not quite come up to the tops.

Bake in a 400°F oven for about 50 minutes or a little longer. The bread should be dark brown and make a hollow sound when tapped on the bottom. If you have even the slightest suspicion that the bottom is still a little soggy, put the loaves back directly on the oven rack and bake them for another few minutes. Cool on racks.

✻ VARIATION ✻

For a somewhat different flavor, try substituting molasses for the honey.

This is another quick, easy, delicious, and nutritious bread. As in all yeast batter breads, the dough is sticky, and it is best to corn-meal the pans after buttering them. The recipe is smaller than the one for No-Knead Whole-Wheat Bread and will make two medium loaves (8 × 4 inches), one round casserole or soufflé-dish loaf, or two 1-pound coffee-can breads. If you use cans, use corn meal on the sides as well as the bottoms.

NO-KNEAD WHEAT-GERM BREAD

	2 tablespoons (2 packets) active dry yeast
½ liter	**2 cups warm water (43–46°C, 110–115°F)**
80 milliliters	**⅓ cup nonfat dry milk powder**
	2 tablespoons honey
	2 tablespoons oil
	2 teaspoons salt
¾ liter	**3 cups whole-wheat flour**
¼ liter	**1 cup wheat germ**

Put all ingredients together in a standard mixing bowl. Use a wooden spoon and beat for a couple of minutes. Cover and put in a warm place to rise, about 45 minutes.

Poke the batter down with your fingers, divide it in half with a knife, and put it into the prepared pans. Cover it and let it rise until it is a little less than double in bulk—for 30 to 35 minutes. Bake at 375°F for 45 minutes or until the bread is well browned and hollow-sounding when tapped. Turn out on wire racks to cool.

FLATBREADS

As you know, in very ancient times, all bread was unleavened, or flat. The Hebrews had sourdough, the Egyptians later developed yeast, and raised bread made its way through most of Europe and to parts of Asia and the New World as well. However, there are many areas where the old-style flatbreads are still favored and are commonly used.

The recipe we begin with is known virtually everywhere, since Jews all over the world use it during the feast of Passover. The Hebrew name for flatbread is *matzoh.* The standard commercial product is factory-made, contains white flour, and comes in squares that are neatly scored (like tablet paper) so that they can easily be broken along the score lines. The version that follows is quite different.

MATZOH

The Bible never gets around to telling us what *kind* of bread the ancient Hebrews had to bake in such a hurry when they fled from Egypt. It seems safe to assume, however, that they had neither white flour nor machinery for making perfect squares, and so the unleavened bread *might* have been something like this. Actually, it is very good, and you don't have to be Jewish or even have a special feast to enjoy it. Break it up and use it instead of crackers. It's excellent to serve with dips—very thin and crisp, but strong enough to hold a good glob of anything.

¼ liter	1 cup water
½ liter	2 cups whole-wheat flour
	2 tablespoons oil
	1 teaspoon salt

Put the water into a standard-size mixing bowl and add the other ingredients. Mix first with a spoon, then with your hand. Knead the dough for a minute or two, just to see if it is firm enough to handle well; if it isn't, add a little more flour.

Form the dough into a ball and cut it in half. Sprinkle a little flour on a board and with a rolling pin roll each piece of dough into a large, thin circle. Put each circle on a baking sheet that has been sprinkled lightly with corn meal.

Bake the matzoh at 375°F for about 40 minutes or a little more; it should be just beginning to turn brown and must be very crisp. When it is thoroughly cool, break it into pieces and store in air-tight tins.

Pita originated in Mesopotamia and is still the common bread of the Middle East. The small round or oval breads puff up when baked, then deflate; when they are split open, there is a space in the center that can be stuffed with a filling.

PITA

A filled pita is a meal that can be eaten on the run, and it is the Middle Eastern equivalent of the American hot dog or hamburger.

You can use pita without filling, just as a bread, and it's perfect to serve with a dip.

	1 tablespoon (1 packet) active dry yeast
	2 teaspoons salt
¼ **liter plus 60 milliliters**	**1¼ cups warm water (43–46°C, 110–115°F)**
	1 tablespoon oil
¾–**1 liter**	**3–4 cups unbleached white flour**

Mix the first four ingredients and 3 cups flour in a regular mixing bowl. Add more flour, a little at a time, until the dough is easy to handle. Knead it until it is smooth and shiny. Put it into an oiled bowl and turn it over, oily side up. Cover the bowl, put it in a warm place, and let the dough rise until it has doubled in bulk.

Punch the dough down, cut it in half, then cut each half into four equal pieces. Form eight balls of dough and let them rest for 10 minutes.

Sprinkle a little flour on a board and use a rolling pin to roll each ball into a circle about ¼ inch thick. Don't be concerned if your circles are irregular; the handmade look is part of their charm.

Put them on lightly oiled baking sheets and let the pitas rise until they have doubled in bulk. Put the pans into a very hot oven —475°F—for about 15 minutes. The pitas are done when they have just *started* to brown. Keep them covered with a towel while they are cooling so that they stay soft. They will lose their puffiness, but when you carefully split one open, you will find a pouch in the center.

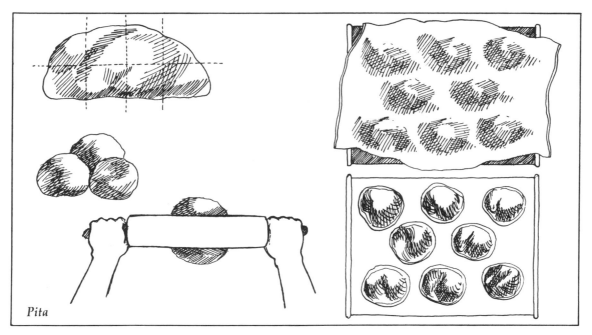

Pita

If you are not going to use your pitas promptly, put them in a plastic bag to keep them soft. If you want to make them ahead of time for a party, you can freeze them very successfully. When you are ready to serve them, let them thaw, then wrap them in aluminum foil and heat them in a 375°F oven for 10 to 15 minutes.

You can stuff pita with just about anything, but here are a couple of good suggestions.

✽✽

BEEF FILLING FOR PITA	oil or butter for sautéing
	1 tablespoon chopped onion
½ kilogram	1 pound chopped beef
	salt and pepper
	1 egg

Put a little oil or butter into a skillet and sauté the onion until it begins to turn yellow. Add the meat and stir until it loses its pink color and the grains are separate.

Add some salt and pepper, taste, and add more if necessary. Add the egg, stir, and cook (while stirring) for another minute or two, until the egg is well mixed with the meat and makes it stick together a little.

If you like, you can add some chopped or crushed garlic, a few spoonfuls of tomato sauce, chopped parsley, oregano, or other herbs when you add the meat.

❦❦

½ liter	**2 cups (one can) cooked chickpeas (garbanzos)**	**HUMMUS FOR PITA**
	juice of 1 lemon	
	1 clove of garlic (or more, to taste), mashed	
	2 tablespoons olive oil	
¼ liter	**1 cup tahini (sesame seed butter)**	
	salt and pepper to taste	
	fresh parsley, chopped	

Drain the chickpeas but save the liquid. Mash the peas with a fork or a potato masher, or put them into a food processor. Add the lemon juice, garlic, oil, tahini, salt and pepper, and enough liquid to make the mixture light and fluffy. Add a small handful of chopped parsley.

Instead of using hummus as a filling, you can use it as a dip. Sprinkle more parsley over the top and let guests tear off pieces of pita to dip into the bowl.

Lavash is good with any food and lends itself especially well to dips or cheese. Break off pieces of the crisp bread and put them in a basket.

Armenians like soft lavash, too, and use it as a wrap-around bread for such fillings as hummus, cheese, or kebabs. To soften lavash, hold it under running water to wet both sides. Shake off the water and wrap the lavash in a towel for ½ hour.

LAVASH (ARMENIAN FLATBREAD)

	1 tablespoon (1 packet) active dry yeast
¼ liter plus 60 milliliters	1¼ cups warm water (43–46°C, 110–115°F)
	4 tablespoons oil
	2 teaspoons salt
	1 teaspoon sugar
1 liter	4 cups unbleached white flour

Mix the first five ingredients and half the flour in a standard mixing bowl. Beat well with a wooden spoon. Add the rest of the flour and knead for 5 minutes, adding a little more flour if necessary.

Put the dough into an oiled bowl and turn it over. Cover it, put it in a warm place, and let it rise until it has doubled in bulk.

Punch the dough down and cut it into four equal parts. Put each one on a lightly floured board and roll it with a rolling pin into a rectangle about 10 × 14 inches, or into a circle about 15 inches in diameter. Place them on ungreased baking sheets and prick them all over with a fork. Put the lavash into a 400°F oven and let it bake until the surface becomes bubbly and the bottom is brown (you

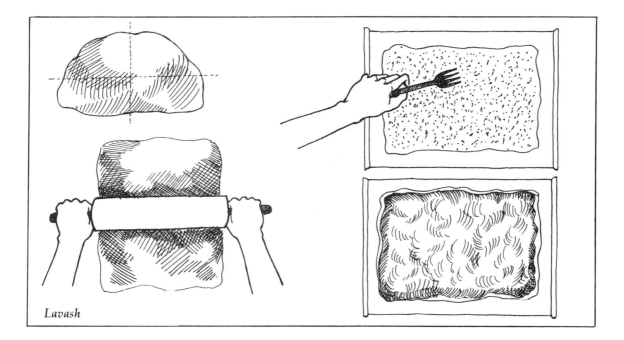

Lavash

can peek with the help of a spatula)—about 20 to 30 minutes. If the top isn't very crisp and brown, slide the pan under the broiler *just for a few seconds.* Keep the door open, the potholder handy—and *watch;* lavash can turn black in a flash. Do the baking in two batches if necessary.

Cool the lavash on racks. Wher. it is cold, break it up and store it in tightly covered tins. It keeps for a long time.

This is an altogether different bread from lavash. It is nice to serve with meals and is particularly appropriate with such specialties as shish kebab or any of the other fine Armenian dishes.

PIDEH (ARMENIAN SEMIFLAT BREAD)

1 liter	4 cups unbleached white flour
	2 teaspoons salt
	1½ tablespoons sugar
	2 tablespoons melted butter
¼ liter	1 cup warm milk
	1 tablespoon (1 packet) active dry yeast
120 milliliters	½ cup warm water (43–46°C, 110–115°F)
	extra melted butter (about 2 tablespoons)

Put the flour, salt, and sugar into a large bowl. Make a hole in the center and pour in everything else except the extra butter. Mix it all together with your fingers and knead for about 5 minutes. Cover the bowl and put it in a warm place until the dough has doubled in bulk. Punch down the dough, knead it for a minute or two, then let it rise a second time.

After the second rising, punch down the dough and cut it in half with a knife. Roll each part into a ball, and then, with a rolling pin, flatten the balls into 8-inch circles. They will be about 1 inch thick.

Butter two round cake tins and put one round in each. Brush the tops with melted butter and let the dough rise until it has doubled in bulk. Bake in a 375°F oven until the breads are golden brown, about 40 to 45 minutes. Turn out on racks to cool.

POORI

India is a country that specializes in flatbreads. This one is traditionally served with curry and other spicy dishes.

Pooris are usually made to order and served hot from the griddle, but it is more practical for the average American cook to make them early in the day or even a day before. As soon as the breads are thoroughly cool, put them in stacks of four or five and wrap each stack in foil. At mealtime, heat them in a hot oven (about 400°F) for a few minutes, unwrap them, and serve promptly.

½ liter	2 cups whole-wheat flour
	2 teaspoons baking powder
	1 teaspoon salt
¼ liter	1 cup cold water
	2 tablespoons oil
	oil for frying

Combine all the ingredients in a medium-size bowl and blend thoroughly. Roll the dough into balls about the size of Ping-Pong balls. Sprinkle a little flour on a board and roll each ball into a circle about ⅛ inch thick.

Put about 1½ inches of oil in a skillet and heat it until it is quite hot, then turn down the heat. Drop in one poori at a time. Hold it under the oil with a spatula or cooking spoon (with a heatproof handle) until the bread is bubbly and puffed. When it is lightly brown, turn it once. Drain it on a paper towel.

Makes 12 to 18, depending on size.

ROLLS

By definition, a roll is a small bread, so a roll can, in fact, be made from any bread dough. From a culinary point of view, however, rolls are generally expected to be somewhat more tender and light than bread, and so, for the finest examples of the art, special recipes are needed. Here is one of the best.

DINNER ROLLS

This recipe makes dinner rolls that are light, tender, delicious, and beautiful. You can shape them to suit yourself, for this one all-purpose recipe will make Pan Rolls, Clover Leaf Rolls, Crescents, Parker House Rolls, Fan Tans, and Love Knots. You can add even more variations if you can invent your own shapes.

180 milliliters	¾ cup warm water (43–46°C, 110–115°F)
120 milliliters	½ cup mashed potatoes (to make from instant potatoes, use warm water for both the water and milk requirements, and omit the butter and seasoning)
	2 tablespoons nonfat dry milk powder
	3 tablespoons sugar
	5 tablespoons butter or margarine, at room temperature
	1 tablespoon (1 packet) active dry yeast
	1 egg
	1 teaspoon salt
¾ liter plus	3 cups or more unbleached white flour
	melted butter (about 3 tablespoons)

Put everything except the flour and melted butter into a large bowl and add 2 cups of flour. Beat well with a wooden spoon. Add 1 cup of flour and begin to knead. Sprinkle more flour on the dough as necessary until it is very easy to handle. Knead for 5 to 7 minutes. Cover the bowl; put it in a warm place, and allow the dough to rise until it has doubled in bulk.

Punch down the dough and follow the instructions below to shape one or more kinds of roll. After forming them, cover the rolls, allow them to rise until they have doubled in bulk, then bake them at 400°F until they have reached the desired shade of brown. Cool them on racks. To keep the tops soft, brush them with melted butter while they are still hot.

᠁᠁

PAN ROLLS

Cut the dough in half and roll each part between your hands to make a rope about a foot long. Cut each rope into twelve pieces of equal size, making a total of twenty-four.

Butter two layer-cake pans. Roll each piece of dough into a ball and arrange twelve of them in each pan. It doesn't matter whether they touch or not; after they are finished, they will all be joined together.

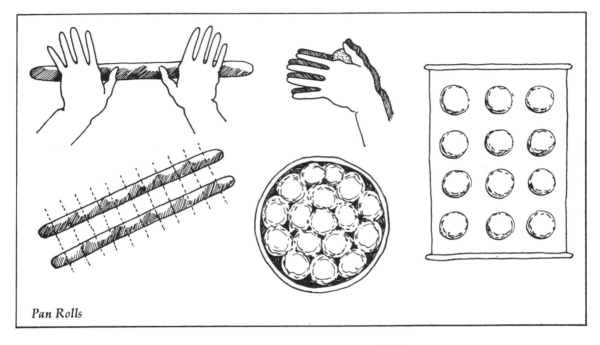

Pan Rolls

𝔀𝔀

CLOVER LEAF ROLLS   Butter twelve muffin cups. Cut the dough in half and roll each half between your hands to form a rope about 18 inches long. Cut each rope into eighteen pieces and roll the pieces into small balls. Place three balls in each muffin cup.

𝔀𝔀

CRESCENTS   Cut the dough in half and with a rolling pin roll each piece into a circle about 8 inches in diameter. With a sharp knife, cut the circle in the shape of a cross, then make two diagonal cuts to form eight equal wedges.

Starting at a curved outside edge, roll up each wedge until the point is just rolled over the top. Curve each roll so that it has a crescent shape. Place them on a buttered baking sheet, allowing plenty of rising space between them.

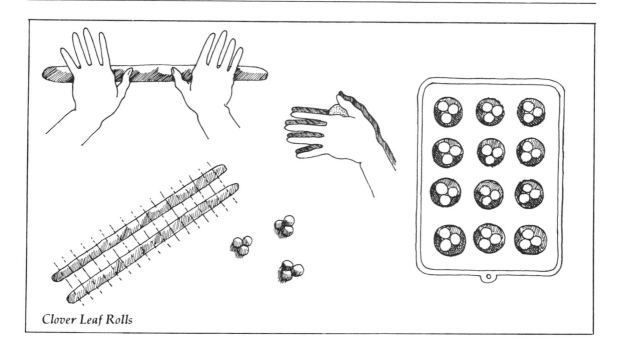

Clover Leaf Rolls

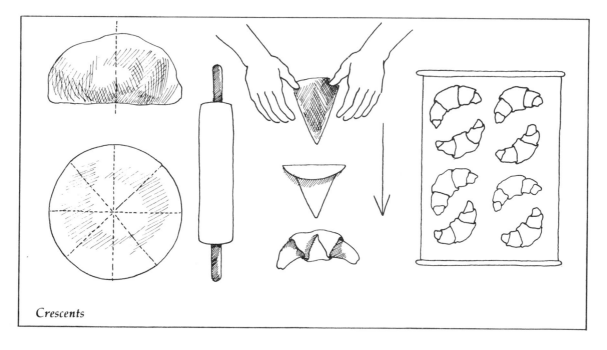

Crescents

PARKER HOUSE ROLLS ❧❧ Cut the dough in half and roll each part into a rectangle about ⅜ inch thick. Use a biscuit-cutter or a floured glass to cut out 3-inch circles. Brush a little melted butter on each one, then fold it over, but not quite in half: the top part should cover only about two thirds of the bottom. Press the edges together, then arrange the rolls at a little distance from each other on a buttered baking sheet.

❧❧

FAN TANS Cut the dough in half and roll each part with a rolling pin into a rectangle about 8 × 16 inches. Brush the tops with melted butter.

Starting at a narrow end, cut each rectangle into five equal strips. Stack the strips; then cut the long strips (still stacked) crosswise into twelve equal parts. Pick up each little stack carefully and put it, cut edges up, into a buttered muffin cup.

❧❧

LOVE KNOTS Cut the dough in half. With your hands, roll each part into a rope as thick as a finger. Cut each rope into 6-inch lengths. Tie each one in a single knot and tuck the ends under. Place at some distance—about a finger's width—from each other on a buttered baking sheet.

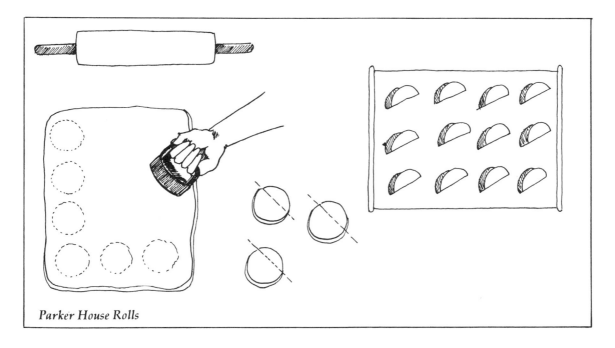

Parker House Rolls

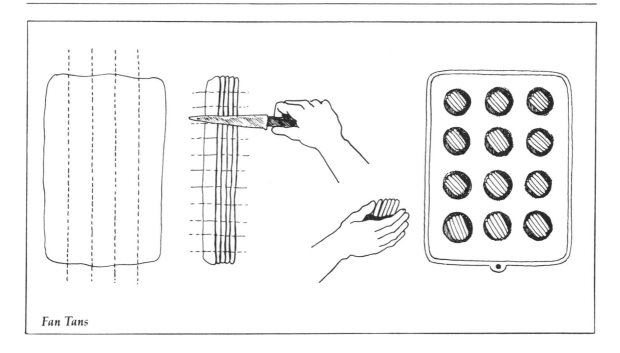

Fan Tans

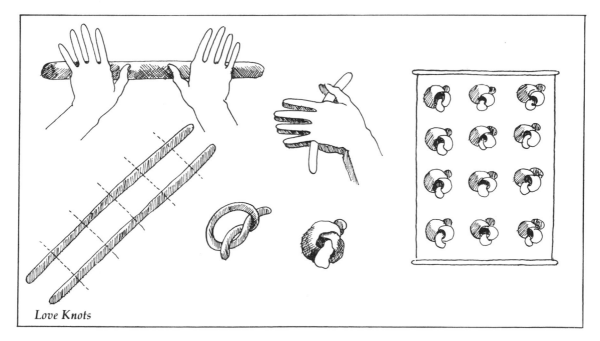

Love Knots

FRENCH-STYLE HARD ROLLS

Lovely Continental-style rolls—hard and crusty on the outside, light and airy inside. Make them round or rectangular.

	1 tablespoon (1 packet) active dry yeast
¼ liter plus 120 milliliters	1½ cups warm water (43–46°C, 110–115°F)
	2 teaspoons salt
¾–1 liter	3–4 cups unbleached white flour
	a little soft butter
	corn meal
	1 egg white mixed with 1 tablespoon cold water

Put the yeast, water, salt, and 3 cups of flour into a mixing bowl. Mix thoroughly, then add as much flour as necessary to make a dough that is stiff enough to handle easily. Knead it until it is smooth, shiny, and bouncy.

Butter the bottom of the bowl and the top of the dough. Cover it and let the dough rise in a warm place until it has doubled in bulk. Punch it down and let it rise a second time.

Punch down the dough again and knead it for a minute or two. Roll it between your hands to form a long rope and cut it into about eighteen equal pieces. Shape the pieces into balls or rectangles—or both—and put them on a baking sheet that has been lightly sprinkled with corn meal.

Brush the rolls with egg-white glaze, then cover them with a dish towel that has been dipped in cold water and tightly wrung out. Let the rolls rise until they are twice their size.

Preheat the oven to 375°F and set a pan of hot water in the bottom. Brush the rolls with the glaze again just before you put them into the oven and once more after the first 15 minutes of baking. Bake for about 30 minutes, or until golden brown. Cool on a wire rack.

WHOLE-WHEAT ROLLS

These rolls don't rise as high as white rolls do, but they have a good wheaty taste and a fine chewy texture. You can shape them as described or divide each one into three finger-thick ropes and braid them.

	1 tablespoon (1 packet) active dry yeast
¼ liter plus 120 milliliters	1½ cups warm water (43–46°C, 110–115°F)
	1 teaspoon salt
	2 tablespoons oil
1–1¼ liters	4–5 cups whole-wheat flour
	a little oil or soft butter

Put the first four ingredients and 4 cups of flour into a mixing bowl. Begin to knead and add more flour if the dough is too sticky to handle. Knead for about 5 minutes, or until the dough is very bouncy.

With a sharp knife, cut the lump of dough in half, then divide each half into six equal parts. Make twelve balls and flatten them with your hand until they are about 1 inch thick.

Use a small, pointy knife to make five cuts, like flower petals, starting almost, but not quite, at the center of each round; there should be an uncut area about the size of a dime in each center.

Put the rolls on a greased baking sheet and brush them with oil or soft butter. Cover them and let them rise until they have doubled in bulk.

Preheat the oven to 350°F and bake the rolls for 25 to 30 minutes, or until they are quite brown on the bottom. Cool on racks.

NOTE: If you want to make rolls that have a finer texture and are a little less chewy, let the dough rise twice—once before you shape the rolls, then again before baking.

SOURDOUGH BREADS

SOURDOUGH

Sourdough is exactly what it sounds like: sour dough. The dough is sour because it has been allowed to ferment, and in so doing has acquired a tangy flavor quite different from that of any regular dough. In addition, since it is left at room temperature and exposed to the air for a long period of time, it becomes a perfect growing medium for the spores of wild yeasts that float around almost everywhere. These yeasts, of varying strains, impart special flavors to the dough, and sourdough bakers often argue about whose bread has the most delicious and distinctive taste.

When the first raised bread was made, back in prehistoric times, it was no doubt because some distracted baker left the dough around too long and it began to ferment accidentally. In all likelihood he or she was scared witless when the stuff began to rise, and surely the delicious flavor of the finished product was attributed to magic.

Whether the baker connected the rising of the dough with its sour flavor, and how many times it had to happen accidentally before someone figured out that it could be done on purpose, we will never know. We *do* know that there are always wild yeasts in clean air, and that, given the right medium and conditions, they'll grow. It's easy enough to provide the medium and conditions, but the tricky part is capturing the yeast.

During the days of the gold rush, every prospector who went West carried a bit of sourdough starter along so that he could bake bread over a campfire. It was a precious item, guarded like gold itself, for while every forty-niner knew how to make new starter (theoretically), it was always a chancy process. It also took more time than any hungry person could reasonably wait.

The formula was simplicity itself: Mix a cup of flour with a cup of milk and set it in the sun to sour. Wait for a wild yeast to settle on the mixture, and if it begins to bubble, you know you've got it. Mix up a batch of dough with it, wait for the dough to rise, then remove one cupful and save it to start the next batch.

Nothing could be easier, right? Wrong, because once in a while the wild yeast just didn't come—or at least it didn't come quickly enough. Innumerable molds can also flourish in flour and milk, and sometimes the mixture turned black, green, or some other unnerving color. When that happened, a miner would walk any number of miles to borrow a little starter from some kindly soul over in the next gulch.

Because the next gulch was often very far away, the prudent prospector made sure that he kept his starter alive under all conditions, even going so far as to wear it under his shirt, hung from a string around his neck. It is said that some of the fine sourdough breads of San Francisco are still made with starters that have been kept going since gold-rush days.

Sourdough bread has a flavor like no other, and a lovely texture. You can buy the starter in most health-food stores, and many companies sell it by mail—but it's much more interesting to start your own.

Try the old prospector method if you want to, but be warned that it is apt to work only in the country (if at all), where the air is pure. In urban areas there are more pollutants than yeasts, but if you have patience, or like to gamble, give it a try. You don't have much to lose.

Put a cup of milk into a glass or crockery container (*no metal* for sourdough) and put it in a warm place to sour. Stir in a cup of white flour and cover it *loosely* with a piece of cloth or a paper towel to keep out flies and the like. Then wait. If you catch some yeast, the mixture will begin to bubble and foam. Stir it once in a while and sniff it to see how sour it smells. When it has a good, really strong aroma, use it, or cover the jar (still no metal, please) and store it in the refrigerator.

If you haven't had any luck within five days, give up. Try it again if you want to—but if you don't, here is a foolproof method, and the one I really recommend.

※ ※

	1 tablespoon (1 packet) active dry yeast	SOURDOUGH STARTER
½ liter	2 cups warm water (43–46°C, 110–115°F)	
½ liter	2 cups unbleached white flour	

Mix all the ingredients in a glass or crockery container. Stir the mixture until it is blended but don't try to make it smooth; the lumps will work themselves out. Cover the crock loosely with a thin piece of cloth (like a handkerchief) and within hours the mixture will begin to bubble. Leave it for several days until it has a strong sour smell. It is normal for a clear yellow liquid to form on top; just stir it back in, once a day. If any other colors appear, you have attracted the wrong organisms; throw it all away, scald the container, and start over.

Once the starter is ready, you can either bake with it right away or store it in the refrigerator for a while. If you do bake right away, you will need only half the starter, so you will still have to refrigerate the rest. Store it in a glass jar or a crock.

If you do *not* plan to bake immediately, divide the starter and put one jar in the refrigerator and another in the freezer, where it will keep for about six months.

Starters improve with age, and once you have a really fine one going, it's a good idea to freeze some just in case the rest of the batch comes to grief. It can happen, because any active strain of yeast needs care and feeding.

Even in the refrigerator, starter remains very slightly active. Within a week or two it will use up all its nutrients and suffocate on the carbon dioxide gas it produces. To prevent this double tragedy, if you don't use your starter for one week, stir it, pour out half and either give or throw it away. Add equal quantities of flour and warm water to fill the container again, let it stay at room temperature overnight, and then refrigerate it again.

Whenever you bake with starter, the procedure is exactly the same. Use one cupful, then add fresh flour and water to the cupful of starter left in the container, stir, leave it out overnight, and store.

If you ever make a really big batch of sourdough bread and want to use all your starter at once, there's no problem. The solution appears in a note in the bread recipe (page 93).

SOURDOUGH BREAD

Sourdough is not a spur-of-the-moment bread. If you want to make it by the classic method, allow a full twenty-four hours—although it may not take that long. Even if your starter is a very potent one, it will be far more whimsical than any commercial yeast could be and remain in the marketplace.

A convenient time to begin a sourdough batch is midafternoon; you will have bread for dinner the next night, but it will be out of the oven before the roast has to go in. Begin the procedure by *setting the sponge,* a fancy term that means giving your starter a good feeding and letting it grow. The longer it sits around, the more sour and tasty your bread will be.

ꙮ

¼ liter	**1 cup sourdough starter**	**THE SPONGE**
½ liter	**2 cups warm water (43–46°C, 110–115°F)**	
¾ liter	**3 cups unbleached white flour**	

Mix all the ingredients together in a medium-size bowl. Cover with plastic wrap and leave at room temperature until the next day.

ꙮ

By the next morning, or at most by early afternoon, the sponge will have doubled its bulk, or more. It will have a bubbly top. (NOTE: If you are out of starter, this is when you can retrieve some. Scoop out a cupful of the sponge and put it into a crock or jar. Add enough flour and water, in about equal parts, to make a total of 2 cups of starter. Cover it loosely and leave it out overnight at room temperature before putting it into the refrigerator.)

THE BREAD

Transfer the sponge from the small bowl to your big one (the dishpan) and add:

	1 tablespoon sugar
	2 tablespoons oil
	1 tablespoon salt
1 liter plus	**4 cups unbleached white flour (use more if needed)**

Be even more careful than usual when adding flour to any sourdough recipe; sourdough starters and sponges vary *very* widely in consistency, so you might need quite a bit more or less flour than specified. Start with half the flour and add more, a little at a time, as you knead. Sourdough takes long kneading—at least 8 or 10 minutes—but it is a very pleasant dough to work with. It quickly becomes smooth and tractable, and it feels really good.

Keep sprinkling little bits of flour over the dough as you knead it until it won't absorb any more. Keep kneading, folding, turning, and kneading some more. If you want to make free-form loaves (without pans), the dough has to be stiff enough to hold its shape. Test it by putting a blob on a greased pan or plate. If it flattens out, you need more flour. If you are going to use pans, it doesn't matter if the dough is a little softer.

Form the dough into a ball, put it into a greased bowl and turn it over. Put a piece of plastic wrap over the top and put the bowl in a warm place. When the dough has nearly doubled in bulk, punch it down and prepare your pans. If you have French-bread pans, use them. If not, make long or round loaves on a flat pan, or shapes for bread pans, coffee cans, or casseroles. It will all be good. Prepare French-bread pans or standard loaf pans by greasing them; a flat pan, for free-form breads, doesn't need to be greased but should be sprinkled lightly with corn meal. If you are using cans or casseroles, grease them *and* sprinkle them with corn meal (sides as well as bottoms) to make sure you have no removal problems.

Cut the dough in half (or in three or more parts if you want small loaves) and shape it. Put the loaves into the pans, cover them, and let them rise in a warm place until they have doubled in bulk. If your starter is a good, active one, this rising should take only about 45 minutes—but sourdough is unpredictable (until you really get to know your own starter), so don't be dismayed if it takes longer. Just be prepared to go along with whatever it does.

When the loaves have risen, slash them with a razor blade or a sharp knife—four diagonal cuts for long loaves, a cross for round ones. Heat the oven to 400°F and put a pan of hot water in the bottom. Paint the bread with cold water that has a little salt in it (about a pinch to a half glass). Repeat the water-painting several times during baking.

Bake the bread for about 50 minutes—or as long as it takes to turn a rich, golden brown with a very heavy crust. If the bottoms aren't as crusty as the tops, put them directly on the oven rack for an extra few minutes of baking. Cool on wire racks.

Sourdough freezes well. When you thaw it, rub it with cold water before heating it in a hot oven to restore the crisp crust.

❧ *VARIATION* ❧

SOURDOUGH WHOLE-WHEAT BREAD

Make the sponge as before, but on the second day, when you make the bread, use whole-wheat flour instead of white.

This is a compromise bread—sourdough starter for flavor, dry yeast for speed. It's not as good as the real thing, but you can make it in a few hours, and with that advantage you may well prefer it.

QUICK SOURDOUGH BREAD

	1 tablespoon (1 packet) active dry yeast
¼ liter plus 120 milliliters	1½ cups warm water (43–46°C, 110–115°F)
¼ liter	1 cup sourdough starter (at room temperature)
	1 tablespoon sugar
	1 tablespoon salt
1½–1¾ liters	6–7 cups unbleached white flour

In a large bowl mix the yeast, water, starter, sugar, salt, and 4 cups of flour. Beat well with a wooden spoon. Cover and leave in a warm place until the dough rises to double its bulk.

Add 2 cups of flour and begin to knead. Add more flour if necessary to keep the dough easy to handle.

Knead for 8 to 10 minutes, until the dough is smooth and shiny, and stiff enough to hold its shape. Cut it in two, and form long or round loaves. Put them on a baking sheet sprinkled with corn meal, cover them, and let them rise in a warm place for 40 minutes.

Slash the loaves as described in the preceding recipe and brush them with cold water. Put the pan into a cold oven. Turn on the oven to 400°F and set a pan of hot water in the bottom. Bake the bread for about 45 minutes, or until it is nut brown. Brush it once or twice with cold water during the baking period.

As soon as the bread is finished, cool it on wire racks.

SOUR RYE BREAD

This is it. The real thing: Jewish Rye, Deli Rye, New York Rye; whatever you call it, it's the kind with a soft inside, crisp crust, and caraway seeds. The only kind of bread in the world that's right with pastrami and a pickle.

❦❦

THE SPONGE

The day or evening before:

¼ liter	1 cup sourdough starter
½ liter	2 cups warm water (43–46°C, 110–115°F)
	4 tablespoons oil
	2 tablespoons molasses
½ liter	2 cups rye flour
½ liter	2 cups unbleached white flour

Don't forget to feed your starter container and leave it out overnight.

Mix the sponge ingredients together in a large bowl. Wet a dish towel, wring it out, and cover the bowl with it. Leave the bowl at ordinary room temperature overnight and for a total of at least 12 hours; it doesn't matter if you leave it longer.

❦❦

THE BREAD

The next day:

	1 tablespoon salt
	½ teaspoon baking soda
¼ liter	1 cup rye flour
	1 tablespoon caraway seeds
½–¾ liter	2–3 cups unbleached white flour
	1 egg white mixed with 1 tablespoon cold water

Stir down the sponge and add the salt, soda, rye flour, seeds, and 2 cups white flour. Stir with a wooden spoon until you can't stir any more, and then begin to knead. Add more flour as necessary to keep the dough from sticking.

This is not an easy dough to handle; rye flour is deficient in gluten and very sticky, so you have to work the white flour extra hard so that its gluten is strong enough to "carry along" the rye flour. Knead for a full 10 minutes and don't cheat. Continue to sprinkle small amounts of white flour over and under the dough to keep it from sticking.

When the dough becomes strong, smooth, and bouncy, divide it into two or three parts. Shape loaves that are oval or round, and place them as far from each other as possible on a baking sheet that has been sprinkled with corn meal.

Make three diagonal slashes on each loaf; cover them and let them rise in a warm place until they have doubled in bulk—about 2 hours.

Preheat the oven to 375°F. Brush the loaves with egg white and water and repeat the glazing after the first ½ hour of baking time. Bake for about 50 minutes, or until the bread sounds hollow when rapped on the bottom. Cool on wire racks.

FESTIVE YEAST BREADS

Virtually all Western peoples bake special breads for special occasions. Many recipes for them can be found in ethnic cookbooks. The recipes that appear here are a few that are popular throughout the United States.

CHALLAH

This is the traditional Jewish Sabbath bread. It graces Jewish tables on Friday nights and also turns up on other special occasions such as holidays, weddings, and bar mitzvahs.

For large gatherings, the recipe is often tripled—or more—and a single challah (the *c* is silent, so it's pronounced *holla*) is made in giant form.

180 milliliters	¾ cup warm water (43–46°C, 110–115°F)
	1 tablespoon (1 packet) active dry yeast
	1 tablespoon sugar
	1 teaspoon salt
	1 tablespoon oil
	1 egg
½–¾ liter	2–3 cups unbleached white flour
	1 egg yolk beaten with 2 tablespoons water
	poppy seeds (optional)

Mix the water, yeast, sugar, salt, oil, egg, and 2 cups of flour in a large bowl. Beat well with a wooden spoon.

Add enough flour to make the dough easy to handle, and begin to knead. Sprinkle with flour if necessary, and continue to knead for about 5 minutes, or until the dough is perfectly smooth and shiny. Put it into a greased bowl and turn it over.

Cover the dough and put it in a warm place to rise until it has doubled in bulk. Punch it down and cut it into four equal parts. Use your hands to roll three of the parts into ropes about a foot long. Put them on a lightly greased baking sheet and pinch them together at one end. Then, working very carefully so as not to stretch the dough, loosely braid the strands. When you come to the end, pinch the ends together, then tuck both ends of the loaf under so that they look neat.

Now divide the remaining piece of dough into three parts and, working just as you did before, make a small braid. Lay it right on top of the big braid, down the center. Lightly brush the whole loaf with oil, then cover it and let it rise until it has doubled in bulk.

Paint the loaf, top and sides, with egg-yolk glaze, and sprinkle it with poppy seeds if you want to. Preheat the oven to 375°F and bake the bread for 25 to 30 minutes, until it is a rich brown on top and bottom. Put it on a wire rack to cool.

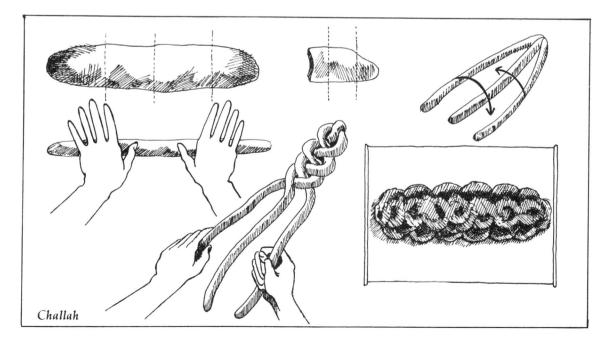

Challah

Fruit bread is a traditional holiday bread of Italy, but this recipe takes a somewhat untraditional form; it is a batter bread and requires no kneading. It is equally good made with white or whole-wheat flour, but either way it is a rich, cakelike bread and should be served as a dessert.

PANETTONE

120 milliliters	½ cup (1 stick) soft butter or margarine
180 milliliters	¾ cup brown sugar
	3 eggs
	2 tablespoons (2 packets) active dry yeast
80 milliliters	⅓ cup nonfat dry milk powder
¼ liter plus 80 milliliters	1⅓ cups warm water (43–46°C, 110–115°F)
	1 teaspoon salt
¾ liter plus 120 milliliters	3½ cups flour (whole-wheat or unbleached white)
	2 teaspoons anise powder
	4 tablespoons currants
	4 tablespoons brandy, rum, or Marsala
¼ liter	1 cup diced, mixed glacé fruit (the kind packaged for fruit cake)
	a little honey and a few blanched almonds (optional)

Cream the butter and sugar together in a large bowl. Separate the eggs and add the yolks to the mixture.

Beat the egg whites until they are stiff enough to stand in peaks, and set them aside.

Add all the other ingredients (except the honey and almonds) to the butter, sugar, and egg yolks in the large bowl and beat well for 2 minutes. Use an electric mixer if you choose.

Fold in the beaten egg whites, cover the bowl and put it in a warm place. When the batter has almost doubled in bulk and is light and frothy (about 1 hour), stir it down.

Pour the batter into a well-buttered 9-inch tube pan or spring form. Let it rise until it reaches the top of the pan.

Preheat the oven to 375°F and bake for 30 minutes. Then, lower the heat to 325°F and bake for another 20 minutes. Test for doneness by sticking a toothpick into the bread; if it comes out gooey, bake a little longer.

After you remove the bread from the oven, let it cool for 5 minutes before removing it from the pan to cool on a rack. At serving time you can leave it plain or you can spread a little honey over the top and decorate it with blanched almonds.

STOLLEN

The traditional German Christmas bread appears here in a particularly rich and fruity version.

❦❦

FRUIT MIXTURE		
	120 milliliters	½ cup raisins
	120 milliliters	½ cup currants
	½ liter	2 cups diced glacé fruits
	120 milliliters	½ cup rum or brandy

Mix all together in a small bowl and let stand for ½ hour. Meanwhile, put out a stick of butter or margarine and 2 eggs to reach room temperature.

❦❦

THE BREAD		
		6 tablespoons (¾ of a stick) soft butter (put rest of stick aside)
	180 milliliters	¾ cup sugar
		2 eggs
		2 tablespoons (2 packets) active dry yeast
		½ teaspoon salt
		1 teaspoon almond extract
	80 milliliters	⅓ cup nonfat dry milk powder
	¼ liter	1 cup warm water (43–46°C, 110–115°F)
	½ liter	2 cups whole-wheat flour
	¾–1 liter	3–4 cups unbleached white flour
	120 milliliters	½ cup sliced or chopped almonds

1 tablespoon grated orange peel
1 tablespoon grated lemon peel
2 tablespoons melted butter
confectioner's sugar

Put the soft butter and sugar into a large bowl and blend them together with a wooden spoon. Add the eggs, yeast, salt, almond extract, milk powder, and water and beat until the mixture is well blended.

Add the whole-wheat flour and 3 cups white flour and begin to knead. Add more flour until the dough is easy to handle. Knead for about 5 minutes, until the dough is smooth and elastic, then cover it and leave it in a warm place to rise until it has doubled in bulk.

Punch down the dough, flatten it out, and with your fingers work in the fruit mixture with its liquid, the almonds, and the grated peels. Press the dough into a rectangle (or two smaller ones if you prefer) and spread the butter left over from the soft stick over the top. Fold one long edge of the rectangle to the center, then fold the other edge so that it overlaps it just a bit. Pinch the seam together and taper the ends neatly. If some of the fruit falls out, just stick it on top.

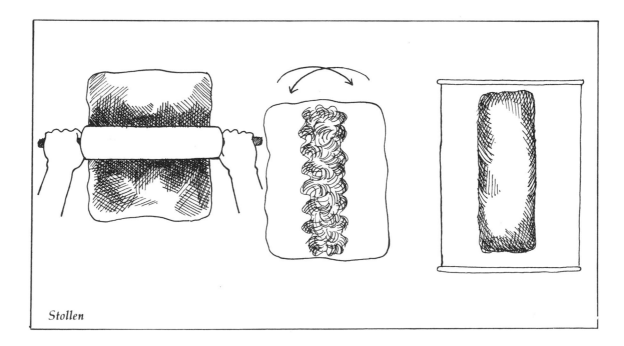

Stollen

Carefully transfer the stollen to a greased baking sheet and let it rise, covered, for one hour. Spread the top with melted butter and bake at 375°F for 40 minutes, or until well browned. Cool in the pan, but while the stollen is still warm, sprinkle it with confectioner's sugar.

KULICH

People of the Russian Orthodox faith celebrate Easter according to a calendar different from ours, and if you know when it falls you can look for these Easter cakes in the windows of Russian bakeries. The tall shape with its covering of white icing makes the kulich look like a snow-covered mountain.

To be truly traditional, save a little dough, form it into a thinner-than-a-pencil roll, and use it to make the initials XV (for *Christ Is Risen*) to put on the top. Some Russians omit the initials and put a fresh red rose on top of the icing instead.

When the bread (which is really more like a cake) is served, the top is cut off in a single slice and replaced, so that even as the loaf grows shorter, it always looks complete.

60 milliliters	¼ cup golden raisins
60 milliliters	¼ cup dark raisins
	2 tablespoons sherry
	6 tablespoons soft butter
120 milliliters	½ cup hot water
60 milliliters	¼ cup sugar
	1 teaspoon salt
	1 egg
	1 tablespoon (1 packet) active dry yeast
	1 teaspoon grated lemon peel
about ¾ liter	about 3 cups unbleached white flour
60 milliliters	¼ cup sliced or chopped almonds

Put the raisins into a small bowl with the sherry and set aside.

Put the butter into a large mixing bowl and add the hot water. Stir with a wooden spoon until the butter is almost melted. Add the sugar, salt, egg, yeast, lemon peel, and about half of the flour. Beat well with a wooden spoon until the mixture is well blended.

Add the soaked raisins with their liquid, the almonds, and a little more flour. Begin to knead and add flour as necessary to keep the dough from sticking. Use as much as—but no more than—you have to. Knead for about 5 minutes, until the dough is bouncy.

Cover the bowl and leave it in a warm place until the dough has doubled in bulk.

Punch down the dough and knead it for about 1 minute. If you are planning to put "XV" on top of the bread, take out a little dough and form the letters. Shape the dough into a ball and drop it into a very well-buttered 2-pound coffee can that has a little corn meal sprinkled in the bottom. Cover the can and let the dough rise until it is just even with the top of the can. Put the "XV" on top.

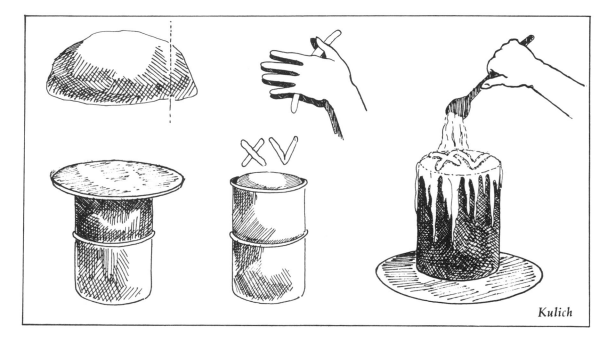

Kulich

Preheat the oven to 350°F and bake the bread for 45 to 50 minutes, until a skewer inserted in the center comes out clean. Turn the bread out of the can and cool it on a rack.

When the kulich is cool, frost it with confectioner's sugar icing, allowing the icing to dribble down the sides.

ἒ ἒ

CONFECTIONER'S SUGAR ICING

| 120 milliliters | ½ cup confectioner's sugar |
| | 1 teaspoon plus several drops milk or cream |

Put the sugar into a small bowl and add a teaspoon of milk or cream. Add more, one drop at a time, until the icing is just thin enough to spread and run down the sides of the kulich. If you make it *too* thin, it will all run off without leaving a nice thick coating on top. If you do accidentally make the icing too runny, just blend in some more sugar until it thickens. Stir it until it is completely smooth.

QUICK BREADS

Although some yeast breads can be made in relatively little time, the term "quick bread" never refers to a yeast bread, but rather to one that is made with baking powder, baking soda, or a combination of the two.

Quick breads are less exciting than yeast breads from the baker's point of view, but they have some very definite advantages. All of them can be prepared in about one hour (and some in much less time than that), they are simple to make, and they run the gamut from meal-accompaniment breads to some that make elegant desserts.

Because they tend to be crumbly, quick breads do not lend themselves well to sandwiches, but most of them make excellent toast.

Since quick breads don't require kneading, you won't need your dishpan for these, but just an ordinary mixing bowl.

YELLOW CORN BREAD

Yellow corn bread is the Northern or Yankee variety—thick, moist, and slightly sweet. It is best baked just before dinner and served steaming hot.

¼ liter	1 cup unbleached white flour
60 milliliters	¼ cup sugar
	4 teaspoons baking powder
	¾ teaspoon salt
¼ liter	1 cup yellow corn meal

¼ liter

1 cup milk
2 eggs
4 tablespoons (½ stick) soft butter
   or margarine

Preheat the oven to 425°F.

Put the flour, sugar, baking powder, and salt into a regular mixing bowl. Add the corn meal, milk, eggs, and butter, and stir hard with a wooden spoon until all the flour is moist. There will be lumps in the batter but don't try to get rid of them. Unlike yeast dough, baking-powder batter should not be handled too much and should be put into the oven as quickly as possible.

Pour the batter into a well-buttered 9-inch square pan. Bake it for 20 to 25 minutes, or until a toothpick inserted in the center comes out clean. Be careful not to overbake since corn bread has a tendency to become dry.

Cut the bread into squares and serve it right from the pan. It makes about 9 average servings.

✴✴

Make the same batter, but spoon it into buttered (or lined) muffin tins. Make each about ⅔ full and bake for 15 to 20 minutes. The recipe will make between 12 and 15 muffins, depending on the size of the tins.

CORN MUFFINS

A tender, crumbly, biscuitlike bread that can be made an hour before mealtime. Break off chunks to serve it, but if there is any left over, slice it for breakfast toast.

SCOTTISH SODA BREAD

½ liter plus 120
   milliliters

2½ cups unbleached
   white flour
2 teaspoons sugar
2 teaspoons baking powder
1 teaspoon baking soda
½ teaspoon salt
3 tablespoons soft butter or
   margarine

¼ liter

1 cup buttermilk
1 tablespoon caraway seeds
   (optional)

Preheat the oven to 375°F and sprinkle a small amount of flour on a round or square cake tin or pie plate.

Put all the dry ingredients into a standard mixing bowl. Add the butter and work it in with your fingertips until the mixture is finely divided into small particles and crumbly. Add the buttermilk and stir just long enough to moisten the dry ingredients. Knead it in the bowl for a minute or so. The purpose of the kneading is not to develop gluten, as with yeast dough, but just to mix the dough thoroughly, so don't overdo it. If the dough is so sticky that it's impossible to handle, add a little bit more flour.

Shape the dough into a ball about 8 inches in diameter and put it on the floured pan. Dip a sharp knife in flour and use it to make two deep cuts on the loaf (almost to the bottom) in the shape of a cross. As the bread bakes, the cuts will spread apart.

Bake for 30 to 40 minutes, until the bread is golden brown and spread out like an open flower.

Cool on a wire rack. To serve, break along the cut lines.

IRISH SODA BREAD

Another soda bread, similar to the Scottish in form, but richer and sweeter. It is better suited to breakfast or teatime than to dinner.

Some experts claim that the Irish country folk always make this bread with whole-wheat flour. Not surprisingly, it makes a somewhat coarser, heavier product, but you might try it and see which version you prefer. Half white, half whole-wheat is recommended rather than all whole-wheat.

1¼ liters	5 cups unbleached white flour
	1 teaspoon salt
	1 teaspoon baking powder
	1 teaspoon baking soda
	4 tablespoons sugar
	4 tablespoons (½ stick) soft butter or margarine
¼ liter plus 180 milliliters	1¾ cups buttermilk
	1 egg
¼ liter	1 cup currants

Preheat the oven to 375°F. Sprinkle a little flour over a large baking sheet.

Put all the dry ingredients into a mixing bowl and work in the butter with your fingertips until the mixture is crumbly and even in texture.

Make a well in the center and pour in the buttermilk. Add the egg and beat well with a wooden spoon to distribute the egg into the buttermilk. Continue to mix with the spoon until all the flour is wet, then knead with your hand just to complete the mixing. Add the currants and mix them in.

Cut the dough in half and shape each half into a ball. Put them on the floured baking sheet at a distance from each other. With a knife dipped in flour after each cut, make a deep cross across each loaf, almost—but not quite—to the bottom.

Bake for about 40 minutes, until golden brown. Cool on wire racks and do not cut until thoroughly cold.

BAKING POWDER BISCUITS

The only secret to turning out light and flaky biscuits is to handle the dough as little as possible. Many cooks have made great reputations because of their biscuits, but it's hard to understand why; biscuits are extremely easy to make and take very little time.

½ liter	2 cups unbleached white flour
	3 teaspoons baking powder
	1 teaspoon salt
	4 tablespoons soft butter (or oil)
180 milliliters	¾ cup cold milk

Preheat the oven to 450°F.

Sift the dry ingredients into a bowl and work in the butter or oil with your fingertips. When the mixture is crumbly, add the milk all at once. Knead the dough *very lightly,* just enough to make it smooth—about 20 strokes.

Put the dough on a lightly floured board; dust a little flour on your hands, and flatten the dough gently until it is about ¾ inch thick. Cut out the biscuits with a floured biscuit-cutter or the edge of a small glass. If you prefer, pat the dough into a rectangle and cut it into squares or diamonds instead.

Place the biscuits on an ungreased baking sheet and bake them for 12 to 15 minutes, until they are golden brown.

꒳ *VARIATIONS* ꒳

CHEESE BISCUITS

Add ½ cup grated Cheddar (or other) cheese when you add the milk.

HERB BISCUITS

Add ¼ teaspoon each of oregano, chives, and basil to the dough. Or, if you prefer, add ¾ teaspoon of a single herb, such as dill weed.

MUFFINS

A batch of muffins can always be whipped up quickly for breakfast, tea, or snacks. There are several variations on this basic recipe, and you can undoubtedly think up many more on your own.

Well-made muffins have a fine texture with no big air tunnels running through them. They are tender and light and have nicely rounded tops. To achieve the best results, put all the dry ingredients into the bowl first (including any nuts, fruits, or the like) and then add the liquid. Stir no more than about a dozen times, leaving the batter lumpy.

Be sure the oven is hot and the muffin pans greased (or lined with fluted muffin papers) before you begin so that you can get your muffins into the oven within seconds of mixing them.

½ liter	2 cups unbleached white flour
	4 teaspoons baking powder
	½ teaspoon salt
	4 tablespoons sugar
	1 egg, slightly beaten
	4 tablespoons melted butter or margarine
¼ liter	1 cup milk

Preheat the oven to 400°F and butter or line the pans.

Sift the flour, baking powder, and salt into a bowl. Stir in the sugar, then add the egg, butter, and milk. Stir *just* enough to moisten the dry ingredients, and spoon the lumpy batter into prepared muffin tins until they are about two-thirds full.

Bake for about 20 minutes, or until the muffins are brown. Makes 12 to 15 muffins, depending on the size of the pans.

彩 *VARIATIONS* 彩

WHOLE-WHEAT MUFFINS

Substitute 1 cup of whole-wheat flour for an equivalent amount of white flour.

BRAN MUFFINS

Substitute 1 cup of bran for an equivalent amount of flour.

BLUEBERRY MUFFINS

Add 1 cup of blueberries (dried between paper towels) to the flour mixture.

DRIED FRUIT MUFFINS

Add ½ cup of chopped dates, prunes, apricots, raisins, figs, or other dried fruit to the flour mixture.

NUT MUFFINS

Add ½ cup of unsalted chopped nuts to the flour mixture.

CORN MUFFINS

See recipe on pages 104–105.

OTHER IDEAS

Among the many other additions you can make to basic muffins are coconut, chocolate bits, candied orange peel, chopped cranberries mixed with a little sugar.

SWEET QUICK BREADS

FRUIT AND HONEY HEALTH LOAF

A sweet, cakelike loaf filled with things that are both good and good for you. It's nice for dessert, for snacks, for afternoon tea, or with a glass of cold milk.

¼ liter	1 cup honey
	2 tablespoons soft butter or margarine
	1 teaspoon salt
	1 egg
180 milliliters	¾ cup buttermilk (substitute plain milk with 1 tablespoon lemon juice if you don't have buttermilk)
½ liter plus 120 milliliters	2½ cups whole wheat flour
60 milliliters	¼ cup bran (or wheat germ)
80 milliliters	⅓ cup raisins
80 milliliters	⅓ cup currants
	1 tablespoon grated orange peel
	1 teaspoon baking soda

Preheat the oven to 300°F and butter a large loaf pan.

Mix the honey and butter with a wooden spoon. Add the salt, egg, and buttermilk, and beat with the spoon until the mixture is well blended. Add the rest of the ingredients and stir just long enough to distribute everything evenly.

Pour the mixture into the pan and bake for 1 hour and 40 minutes, or until the loaf is very brown and is beginning to shrink away from the sides of the pan. Cool before cutting.

DATE AND BRAN LOAF

Another sweet but wholesome bread. It is particularly good with cream cheese.

¼ liter plus 120 milliliters	1½ cups chopped dates (a ¼-kilogram or 8-ounce package)
120 milliliters	½ cup raisins
½ liter	2 cups boiling water

	2 eggs
180 milliliters	¾ cup brown sugar
½ liter	2 cups whole-wheat flour
½ liter	2 cups bran (pure bran, not the prepared cereal)
¼ liter	1 cup chopped nuts (walnuts or pecans)
	1 teaspoon vanilla
	2 teaspoons baking powder
	1 teaspoon baking soda

Preheat the oven to 350°F. Butter two medium-size or three small loaf pans.

Put the dates and raisins into a small bowl and pour the boiling water over them.

Break the eggs into a mixing bowl and stir in all the other ingredients. Add the dates and raisins with their liquid last. Do not beat, but just stir until everything is well mixed.

Divide the batter into the pans and bake for about 45 minutes, or until a toothpick inserted into the center of a loaf comes out clean. Cool before cutting.

CRANBERRY NUT BREAD

A moist, rich, slightly sweet fruit bread that makes an appropriate small gift at Thanksgiving or Christmas time. If you store cranberries in your freezer when they are in season, do not thaw them before chopping.

½ liter	2 cups fresh or frozen cranberries, coarsely chopped (in a chopping bowl or food processor)
120 milliliters	½ cup chopped walnuts
¼ liter	1 cup sugar
½ liter	2 cups whole-wheat flour
	1 teaspoon salt
60 milliliters	¼ cup oil
180 milliliters	¾ cup orange juice
	1 tablespoon grated orange peel
	1 egg
	1½ teaspoons baking powder
	½ teaspoon baking soda

Preheat the oven to 350°F and butter two medium-size or three small loaf pans.

Put all the ingredients into a mixing bowl and stir with a wooden spoon until blended. Do not beat.

Divide the batter into the pans and bake for about 1 hour, or until a toothpick inserted into the center of a loaf comes out clean. Cool the bread on racks and do not cut until it is cold. It will keep for days in the refrigerator and freezes very well.

CARROT BREAD

A rich, sweet, spicy dessert bread. It keeps for a long time in the refrigerator and freezes perfectly.

	4 eggs
¼ liter plus 120 milliliters	1½ cups sugar
½ liter	2 cups finely shredded raw carrots
¼ liter plus 60 milliliters	1¼ cups oil
¾ liter	3 cups whole-wheat flour
	2 teaspoons baking powder
	1½ teaspoons baking soda
	¼ teaspoon salt
	2 teaspoons cinnamon (or pumpkin-pie spice)

Preheat the oven to 350°F and butter two large loaf pans.

Beat the eggs and sugar together in a mixing bowl. Add all the remaining ingredients and stir until they are well blended.

Turn the batter into the pans and bake for 1 hour, or until a toothpick inserted into the center of a loaf comes out clean. Cool in the pans on wire racks.

🌿 VARIATIONS 🌿

CARROT-NUT BREAD

Add 1 cup of coarsely chopped walnuts to the batter.

ZUCCHINI BREAD

Substitute shredded raw zucchini for the carrots, and add 1 teaspoon of vanilla and an extra teaspoon of cinnamon.

This is one of the best of all fruit breads—really a cake in bread's clothing. Served with a dollop of whipped cream, it makes an appropriate and elegant close to a Thanksgiving dinner—and a change from the ubiquitous pie. You can safely make it weeks ahead of time and keep it in the freezer.

Use a fresh pumpkin if it's that time of year and you happen to have one. If not, canned pumpkin does the job perfectly and certainly saves time and trouble.

PUMPKIN BREAD

¾ liter	3 cups cooked and mashed pumpkin (or one 822-gram or 29-ounce can)
¼ liter	1 cup honey
¼ liter	1 cup brown sugar
¼ liter	1 cup oil
¼ liter	1 cup chopped walnuts
	1 teaspoon salt
	1 teaspoon ground cloves
	1 teaspoon cinnamon
	4 teaspoons baking soda
½ liter	2 cups unbleached white flour
½ liter plus 120 milliliters	2½ cups whole-wheat flour
120 milliliters	½ cup wheat germ

Preheat the oven to 350°F and butter two large loaf pans.

Mix all the ingredients together in a mixing bowl. When they are thoroughly blended, divide the batter into the pans. Bake for 1 hour, or until a toothpick inserted into the center of a loaf comes out clean. Cool in the pans on wire racks. When the breads are cool, turn them out of the pans and wrap them in foil or plastic wrap.

ODDS AND ENDS

The recipes that follow do not, strictly speaking, fit into a bread book of such modest proportions as this one. They are all, however, forms of bread, fun to make, and recipes you aren't likely to run into every day.

BAGELS   Water bagels are those Jewish hard rolls with a hole in the middle that are famous as a vehicle for lox (smoked salmon) and cream cheese. They're good even if you skip the lox and cheese. Serve them warm, fresh from the oven, split and toasted, or buttered and broiled for a minute.

	1 tablespoon (1 packet) active dry yeast
¼ liter	1 cup warm water (43–46°C, 110–115°F)
	1 tablespoon sugar
	1½ teaspoons salt
½ liter plus 180 milliliters	1¾ cups unbleached white flour

Mix all the ingredients in a bowl. Knead the dough until it is smooth, about 10 minutes, adding a little more flour if necessary to keep it from sticking. Put it into a greased bowl and turn it over. Cover the bowl and let the dough rise until it has doubled in bulk.

Punch down the dough and cut it into eight equal portions. Dust your hands with a little flour and roll each piece of dough into a rope about 6 inches long. Join the ends by pinching them together to form a circle; if necessary, use a drop of water to make them

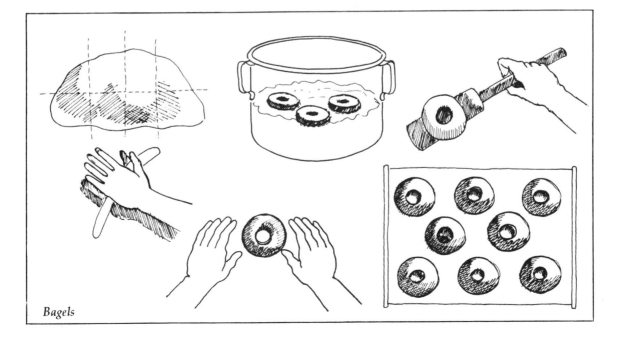

Bagels

stick. Put them on a tray that has been very lightly dusted with flour; cover them, and let them rise for 20 minutes.

While waiting, put about 6 inches of water into the largest pot you can find, and put it on to boil. Reduce the heat so that the water boils gently.

Lift each bagel carefully with a pancake spatula and slide it into the boiling water. If the diameter of the pot isn't large enough to hold all the bagels at once without crowding, boil them in several batches.

Boil the bagels on one side for 3 minutes, then turn them over and cook the other side for 3 minutes. Lift them out and put them on a folded towel to drain for a minute or so.

Transfer the bagels to a greased baking sheet and bake them at 375°F for 30 to 35 minutes, until they are golden brown.

✿ *VARIATION* ✿

EGG BAGELS

Real bagel fans look down upon egg bagels as a modern imitation of the real thing. Egg bagels do, however, have their following, so for those who prefer a richer, less chewy model, here are the changes to make in the basic recipe.

To the original list of ingredients, add 2 eggs, and 2 tablespoons of oil, and increase the amount of flour to 4 cups. Proceed as with water bagels, but when it is time to cut up the dough, divide it into sixteen parts instead of eight.

Add 1 tablespoon of sugar to the boiling water and boil the bagels for 2 minutes on each side instead of 3. Just before you put them into the oven, brush each one with an egg that has been beaten with 1 tablespoon of water.

SOFT PRETZELS

These are the big, soft, fat pretzels that seem to be sold only at carnivals, circuses, ball games—and by venders with carts on city street corners.

In many areas they seem to have totally vanished from the scene, but do not despair—you can still make your own.

Gourmet tip: When I was a child in Philadelphia I bought a pretzel nearly every day at recess time from the old man who sold them at the schoolyard gate. He spread each one with bright yellow mustard (from a slightly rusty can with a wooden paddle in it) for a true taste sensation. If you've never had a soft pretzel with mustard, try it!

	1 tablespoon (1 packet) active dry yeast
	1 teaspoon sugar
	1 teaspoon salt
¼ liter plus 120 milliliters	1½ cups warm water (43–46°C, 110–115°F)
¾–1 liter	3–4 cups unbleached white flour
	1 egg beaten with 1 teaspoon of cold water
	kosher salt

Mix the yeast, sugar, regular salt, and water in a bowl. Add 2 cups of flour and beat well with a wooden spoon. Add more flour until you can easily handle the dough. Knead it until it is smooth and bouncy, about 5 minutes.

Put the dough into a greased bowl and turn it greased side up. Cover it and put it in a warm place until the dough has risen to twice its bulk.

Punch down the dough and cut it into either twelve or sixteen

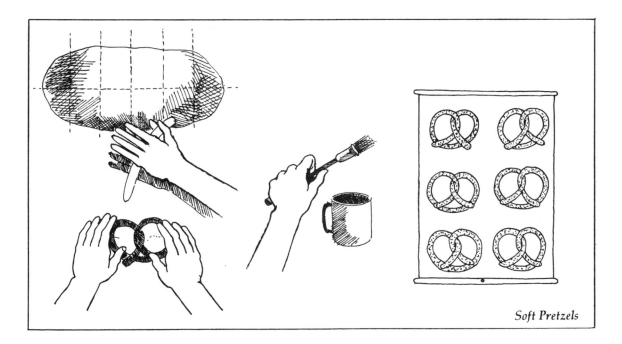

Soft Pretzels

parts, depending on whether you want reasonable-size pretzels or really fat ones (really fat ones are better). Roll each piece of dough into a rope and twist it into a pretzel shape. A little investigation will show you that there is more than one way to twist a pretzel; one of the simpler ways is to tie a single knot and then pinch the loose ends together. If you want to do something more intricate, go ahead. A light dusting of flour on your hands at all times will make the job simpler.

Put the pretzels on a lightly greased baking sheet, leaving room for expansion. Cover them, and let them rise for 20 minutes.

Heat the oven to 425°F. Paint each pretzel with the egg glaze and sprinkle it with kosher salt. Bake for 15 to 20 minutes, or until the pretzels are the desired shade of golden brown. Cool on racks, then store in tins or plastic bags.

It's perfectly all right to bake the pretzels in several batches; the extra rising time won't do them any great harm.

A wholesome, nutritious treat for the baby who has everything (except all its teeth). Tailor the biscuits to the size of the hand that will hold them.

BABIES' TEETHING BISCUITS

¼ liter

1 cup whole-wheat flour
2 tablespoons nonfat dry milk powder
2 tablespoons honey
2 tablespoons oil
1 egg yolk
1 tablespoon water

Mix all the ingredients together. The dough should have the consistency of clay so that you can shape it easily. If it is too crumbly to stick together, add a few drops of water; if it is too sticky, add a little more flour.

Take a pinch of dough about the size of a marble, and shape it into a finger-size biscuit. Leave the biscuits rounded, or flatten them somewhat, as you prefer.

Put them on a lightly greased baking sheet, and bake them at 350°F for 15 minutes. When the biscuits are completely cool, store them in an airtight jar.

Index